THE
WORLD
CUP

AN ESSENTIAL GUIDE
TO MEXICO '86

THE
WORLD
CUP

AN ESSENTIAL GUIDE
TO MEXICO '86

EDITED BY
JULIE WELCH

First published in Great Britain in 1986 by Virgin Books,
328 Kensal Road, London W10 5XJ

Copyright © 1986 by Julie Welch

ISBN 0 86369 147 1

Printed and bound in Great Britain by R. J. Acford, Chichester

Typeset by Keyline Graphics, London NW6

Cover and design by Sue Walliker and Ursula Shaw

Distributed by Arrow Books

The cover photos were kindly provided by Stewart Kendall/Sportsphoto;
Sporting Pictures (UK) Ltd; and Bob Thomas Sports Photography.

Inside illustrations were provided by AllSport Photographic; Bob Thomas
Sports Photography; Associated Press Photos; Photosource; Sport & General;
Sportapics Ltd; Sportsphoto; Sporting Pictures (UK) Ltd.

This book is for Freddy Konynenburg

Nothing would have been possible without Cat Ledger of Virgin, whose hard work and enthusiasm got everything off the ground and kept it there. A debt of gratitude is owed also to *World Soccer* magazine, an invaluable source of reference material, and to my husband Ronald Atkin who, as always, provided the essential nagging, advice and practical help, as well as holding the baby a lot.

CONTENTS

What it's all about: the FIFA World Cup Trophy

A TOURNAMENT OF LOST MINDS AND MARBLES

DAVID RANDALL

This is the time when every newspaper, magazine and guide likes to fill you in on the history of the World Cup. But what you usually get is the boring version. Now, for the first time, we can exclusively present David Randall's Unofficial History of the World Cup . . .

In 1928 the men who run FIFA had an idea. What the game needs, they thought, is a competition to decide which is the best footballing nation on earth; a tournament that would bring together all the world's finest players and, under the supervision of the most august and wise referees, pit them against each other in a spirit of international brotherhood, peace and understanding.

What a shame it was that they couldn't quite pull it off. Instead we got the World Cup. Not, of course, that there haven't been passages of brilliant football, the odd flicker of commonsense from behind the referees' glasses and, although it has hardly been encouraged, fleeting moments of sportsmanship. It's just that there has always been another side to the World Cup: a strange, bizarre, often farcical, and at times even darker, side. No event in sport, it seems, has inspired the loss of marbles on such a global scale as the tournament which the stout little optimists of FIFA began nearly 60 years ago.

They chose for its inauguration the small South American republic of Uruguay, whose chief claims to fame were political instability and the meat factory at Fray Bentos. The football world responded to this news with devastating indifference and with only two months to go no one had entered. But the Uruguayans had a way with people who were reluctant; it was called bribery. They offered to pay everyone's expenses and, miraculously, football associations started to have second thoughts. Powerful forces were now being brought to bear. In Romania King Carol was at work. He was an enlightened ruler whose first act on ascending the throne was to grant an amnesty to all suspended footballers and now he personally contacted the employers of all Romania's players to make sure the lads would get time off for the new tournament. He knew who the players were because he had picked them himself.

Pity about the Argentine president. Jules Rimet presents the inaugural 1930 World Cup Trophy to Dr Paul Jude of the Uruguayan FA

Meanwhile, in downtown Montevideo, swarms of Uruguayans had been engaged to work on the new arena. It was to be called the Centenary Stadium, which was about how long everyone expected its construction would take. But after just eight months it was finished and it was here, on 18 July 1930, that the tournament kicked off. Soon the World Cup had acquired its first hero. He was the United States trainer, an excitable fellow who, in the match against Argentina, took grave exception to a decision against his team, ran onto the pitch and began waving his arms about and haranguing the referee. His diatribe continued until, with a final theatrical flourish, he brought it to a climax by flinging down his little bag of medicaments. This was a mistake, for his dramatic gesture had smashed the bag's principal contents, an economy-sized bottle of chloroform and its soporific vapours now engulfed him. First he lost his thread, then his voice and, finally, all but consciousness. His near-comatose body was then borne back to the sideline where it belonged.

This was not the first time that a referee's decision had unfurled a strange sequence of events, for the standard of officiating in that World Cup was decidedly eccentric. It seemed that from the first whistle the little men in black had been desperately wracking their brains for ways to upstage each other. In Argentina v France, Mr Alemida Rego of Brazil had pulled a brilliant stroke by ending the game six minutes early and the effects must have exceeded his wildest dreams. Delirious Argentine supporters invaded the field, angry French players mobbed Rego, who then tapped his watch, held it up to his ear, consulted his linesmen, recalled the French and decided on a restart – whereupon the Argentine inside-left Cierro promptly fainted. Other referees were not to be outdone. In their next game Argentina beat Mexico 6–3 and most of the credit for this high-scoring affair must go to one Ulysses Saucedo, a fastidious little official who somehow managed to award five penalties. Meanwhile, another referee, given nominal charge of Chile v Argentina, had such spectacular success with his policy of laissez-faire that eventually the Uruguayan police had to mount a full-scale charge to break up the fighting players.

For the final between Argentina and Uruguay, FIFA fortunately managed to find a referee who only *looked* daft. He was a Belgian and took to the field wearing plus-fours, a red striped tie and a deerstalker hat. In other respects the occasion was much as one might have expected – death threats to the officials, an armed guard for both teams, soldiers with fixed bayonets encircling the stadium, neither side able to agree on the match ball (in the end they compromised on one half with each ball) and the Argentine supporters chanting 'Victory or Death'. However, after Argentina's 4–2 defeat everyone calmed down and all that happened was that a rampaging mob stoned the Uruguayan consulate in Buenos Aires, the Argentine President was overthrown and relations between the two finalists' FAs were broken off and not resumed for seven years.

It was now clear that to win the World Cup you needed South Americans in your team – even if your country was in Europe. So when Italy, the hosts,

Italy take the 1938 cup thanks to the world's ugliest cheerleader

lined up for the 1934 tournament, they had three, including Monti, Argentina's centre-half in the 1930 final. They also had the world's ugliest cheerleader, Il Duce, who taught the team to perform a strange salute before each game. The Italian crowds, too, were embarrassingly over the top, baying with a brand of nationalism that might have been said to be more suited to a Fascist rally, were it not for the fact that this is precisely what most of them thought they were attending. The referees were behind them as well and one, a M. Marcet, was so sympathetic to their cause that he was later suspended by his national federation. With all this support, the Italians took the cup.

By 1938 they were down to only one Latin in their side; but the Germans had been making notes. Aware that his country's World Cup squad needed strengthening, Adolf Hitler invaded Austria. When the Germans took the field in France, there among them were four Austrians. For once even Switzerland could not remain neutral and they beat the Teutonic All-Stars 4–2 in the first round. The Germans clearly had a lot to learn about World Cup football, as did Poland who adopted a sporting approach, lost 6–5 to Brazil and then even sent their conquerors a good luck telegram for the quarter-finals. The results of Brazil's next game were more in keeping with the spirit of the event – three men sent off, one broken leg, a broken arm, a host of minor injuries and a draw. But the Brazilian manager did not panic. He only made nine changes for the replay and, having won that, obviously thought he had stumbled on a winning strategy. For the semi-final he made eight changes, including the dropping of his two star forwards, Leonidas and Tim. 'They are,' he explained, 'being rested for the final.' Sure enough, when it came to the final they were rested, as were the rest of the Brazilian squad after their 2–1 semi-final defeat. Italy retained the cup.

Thus far the World Cup had lacked the one element which was to provide more harmless mirth and entertainment than any other in the post-War years – Scotland. Now in 1950, accompanied by the now-traditional skirl of self-inflated pipes and egos, they entered, only to withdraw again as soon as they qualified. It was a brilliant ploy, which allowed England to go off to Brazil and humiliation and demented men in Glasgow bars to claim a moral victory for the next four years. England's shame, of course, came at the hands of the United States and when the absurd result of 0–1 was flashed to Fleet Street, one newspaper took it as an error and actually printed it as 10–1. The final, deciding match of that tournament was between Uruguay and hosts Brazil, and the South American continent took it in its usual nonchalant stride. Gambling mania seized Rio, Brazil were made 10–1 on favourites, the team was promised a £10,000 a man win-bonus and a celebratory samba called 'Brazil the Victors' was composed. It was never performed. Uruguay won the final and three of their supporters died of heart attacks while listening to a radio commentary of the game.

Four years later came the match between Brazil and Hungary which, even in the annals of the World Cup, still stands out for unbridled acrimony and psychopathic violence. Readers are therefore advised that the following narrative is not suitable for those of a nervous disposition. It was, in fact, as early as the third minute that the unwholesome nature of the match was set, when Hidegkuti scored for Hungary and was promptly mobbed by the Brazilians, who then tore off his shorts. The tackles rose higher and higher, retaliation became ever more certain and there was a penalty at each end. Somehow the first half was concluded without the infliction of anything more serious than flesh-wounds but then, after the interval, things began to turn ugly. Santo and Boszic (a Hungarian Member of Parliament) were sent off for fighting, at which point the Brazilian trainer ran on to protest, the Swiss police ran on to remove him and the photographers ran on to record the happy scene. Brazil's Tozzi was next to go, but not before he had delayed his departure somewhat by falling to his knees in front of the referee and begging to be allowed to stay. He finally slunk off weeping to the dressing room, where he was later joined by his colleagues at the end of their 4–2 defeat. But the fight had not gone out of them yet. The lights were turned off in the tunnel, the Brazilians invaded the Hungarian dressing room wielding sticks and bottles and soon a pitched battle was in progress. When order was finally restored, Gustav Sebes was left knocked out, Pinheiro had been cut by a bottle and several others needed treatment.

Naturally the world had relied on Scotland to introduce a note of levity into that tournament and they didn't fail, striking deep into their reserves of native ingenuity to make a complete pig's ear of it all. The Scottish FA, in

Berne '54: Didi of Brazil, and Lantos of Hungary caught in relatively mild mood

Stockholm '58: Kalie Svensson of Sweden and Pele head for the clouds

particular, rose to the big occasion superbly, devising a selection system which ruled out of the finals their captain and linchpin George Young. Even so, they only lost their opening game to Austria by one goal. Clearly further demoralisation was required. It arrived just in time, manager Andy Beattie responding to his nation's hour of need by rowing with the SFA's officials and resigning on the eve of the Uruguay game. It worked a treat. Scotland lost 7–0 and returned home to inaugurate the first of many such inquests. But for once the Scots were not alone in their recriminations. Yet again the format of the competition had been altered to create maximum confusion and Hungary, having beaten the Germans 8–3 in the first round, then lost the final to them by the odd goal in five.

It was now the turn of Brazil to dominate the competition. After the unseemly incidents in Berne they took the precaution of adding a resident psychologist to their squad. He was with them in Sweden in 1958, spending most of his time trying to analyse his players' doodles while the rest of the teams tried to understand the patterns that these bewildering men were making out on the pitch. With the brief exception of Sweden no one could and the Brazilians triumphed. They repeated their victory in 1962 and came to England in 1966 so confident that they would win the trophy for a third time, and therefore outright, that they actually had another made to donate in its place, to be known as the Winston Churchill Cup. It was not needed. Brazil and Pele were kicked off Goodison Park and the finals instead belonged to Alf Ramsey and England. Thanks to a Russian linesman who was able to spot at 50 paces a Hurst goal whose legitimacy has since defied 20 years of scientific and photographic analysis, England won.

The next disputed goal in the World Cup, which came in the 1969 qualifying play-off between El Salvador and Honduras, had rather more complicated consequences. Relations between the two countries had been a bit rocky for some time and four days before the match diplomatic ties were dramatically severed. This, however, was as nothing compared with the aftermath of El Salvador's 3–2 extra-time victory, for within 24 hours of the whistle war had broken out. Three days of bitter fighting then followed which left 3,000 dead and El Salvador £4 million worse off. The finals were necessarily something of an anti-climax for them and they played through their group without a win or even a point. Brazil, however, were busy proving how important a manager is to a great team by romping to a third victory, led by a man who had been in the job barely three weeks.

In terms of bizarre incident and skulduggery it had been a strangely subdued World Cup, as was the one in West Germany that followed it. The hosts won and the tournament was enlivened only by the magnificent gall of the Zaire delegation. At the start of the finals a German company had presented to each squad a luxurious coach, done out in their team colours and designed for their exclusive use during the tournament. After Zaire were eliminated a representative of the company called at their camp to reclaim the vehicle, only to be told that they had already left and were at this very moment speeding happily down the autobahn towards Africa in their well-appointed new charabanc. Only the efficiency of the local Polizei prevented them reaching the border.

It was plain that for a really entertaining World Cup you needed Scotland to be on top form and in 1978 they were, surpassing even themselves. Inspired by manager Ally Macleod's repeated assurances that they would be champions, Scotland strode out for their first game against Peru, missed a penalty and lost 3–1. Macleod was defiant. His message to the World Cup was: 'We will win.' But the World Cup had a message for him: 'What is this Fencamfamin substance we have found in Willie Johnston?' Protesting that the drug was only for the relief of his hay fever, Johnston flew home.

Meanwhile, back in Cordoba, Macleod sent out his team against Iran. 'We will win,' he told them. They drew 1–1. Macleod was now speechless and his team responded to this unexpected boost by beating Holland 3–2. But it was too late and the way was now clear for Argentina to win the cup. This triumph, however, was not without its contentious moments. To progress into the final Argentina needed to beat Peru by four clear goals and just because they won 6–0 and Quiroga, the Peruvian goalkeeper, was born in Argentina, some nasty, suspicious minds implied that there was something dodgy about the result. Quiroga even had to publish an open letter defending himself against corruption charges. Those of us in the know, however, had never doubted him. Any goalkeeper who was booked earlier in the tournament, as he was, for rugby-tackling Poland's Lato in the Polish half of the field, is entitled to be above suspicion.

London '66: Bobby Moore, Gordon Banks and George Cohen on a day that our boys got it right

Mexico '70. Brazil's Zagalo (coach), Carlos Alberto and Fontana flash the Jules Rimet Cup

Buenos Aires '78: Argentine captain Daniel Passarella appears to have heard the name Quiroga once too often

Following these fun and games, Spain and 1982 was almost a let-down. Apart from Italy winning the cup yet failing to beat Cameroon, El Salvador becoming the first side to concede double figures in a finals game, Kuwait's melodramatic protests and West Germany and Austria's convivial and convenient 0–0 draw, nothing out of the ordinary happened. The weirdos stayed at home, the referees appeared to know the rules, Scotland avoided disaster and the kind of strange characters who had so entertainingly populated the previous eleven tournaments were conspicuously absent. Some officials, of course, would like to see the same kind of anodyne contest in Mexico this year. But one rather hopes not. After all, it might be sport but it would hardly be the World Cup.

'ROBSON MUST GET IT RIGHT'

Sir Alf Ramsey was a national hero when he led England to win the World Cup in 1966, before coming a cropper in Mexico in 1970. In this interview with Nigel Clarke of the Mirror *he analyses the problems facing Bobby Robson in Mexico.*

I was ridiculed and then reviled for producing a World Cup team that didn't use wingers. Ramsey's Wingless Wonders, they were called. But England triumphed in the World Cup, and my tactical thinking on the use of the players that I had has revolutionised the game. I believe you don't pick players to fill a position, you just make use of those you have in the best possible way. I didn't finalise my 1966 side until perhaps a month before the championship began. Right now I'm not surprised that Bobby Robson has very little idea of what his line-up will be. And that's because he has problems. Perhaps he won't play with a centre-forward, and use a 4–4–2 formation instead. Twenty years ago, England didn't use a centre-forward until the quarter-final match with Argentina.

Robson still has time, but has he the players? I don't think so. After Peter Shilton we just don't have a second-string goalkeeper. Neither Gary Bailey nor Chris Woods is good enough. In defence the only players I like are Gary Stevens, Terry Butcher and Kenny Sansom.

Bryan Robson will be the key man in midfield so long as he's fit, but I wouldn't give Ray Wilkins a game, and there are massive question marks against Glenn Hoddle and Peter Reid. Up front Chris Waddle and John Barnes promise more than they produce. It's the end of the road for Trevor Francis, and I don't much like Tony Woodcock. Kerry Dixon is not good enough because his control would let him down, while Mark Hateley doesn't score enough goals. Only Gary Lineker looks sharp and effective.

I saw England against Romania at Wembley. We did not play well. Technically we were inferior to a side that couldn't even qualify for Mexico.

Out there where the heat will be stifling and the altitude exhausting you must treat the ball like gold-dust. Possession is so important, we must have players in the side who can hold it when they get it. Quality is so vital.

After that I would be looking for good old-fashioned guts. If Robson is to

The glory days: Sir Alf Ramsey in speculative mood as he pursues a World Cup dream

A study in urgency: Bobby Robson roars his squad on to Mexico

play with three up front, and he's said he'll use a wide man, that will be hard. Whoever gets the job will be in constant action, up and down the flank, working hard, keeping the ball. That will not only be difficult but demanding as well. The man who is prepared to go through the pain barrier is the player I'd pick. So in my opinion England only have six players who are certainties – if fit. Shilton, Stevens, Butcher, Sansom, Robson and Lineker. The door is open for another half-dozen players to come through, just as they did in 1966.

Nobby Stiles was recommended to me by Sir Matt Busby, then manager of Manchester United. I wanted someone to sit in front of the back four, and pick off anything that came through. I tried Nobby in that role, just three months before the World Cup began, in an 'Under-23' international against Scotland in Glasgow. He did it magnificently. The jigsaw was beginning to fall into place. I was always going to use Bobby Charlton coming from behind because he was quick, had two great feet, and explosive shooting. But I wasn't sure about Martin Peters. At one stage I had virtually decided to leave him out. Then I went to West Ham for a match and just concentrated on him for 90 minutes. I then saw what he was able to accomplish.

So we had Charlton who could attack from deep positions and score goals, Peters the one player who could knock in killer balls, Alan Ball who was all industry harnessed to great skill and awareness, and Stiles who could stifle things before they reached the back four. Roger Hunt was called clumsy, but he had better skill and control than Kerry Dixon, and was a very underestimated player. Jimmy Greaves was up front, and I also used John Connolly and Terry Paine, and it wasn't until Jimmy got injured that I finally completed the puzzle. He hurt a shin against France, but still could have played against Argentina. But I put in Geoff Hurst, and he did so well I couldn't leave him out for the semi-final against Portugal even though Greaves was by then fully fit and a proven goalscorer.

England won the World Cup, but it had started a year earlier, when I looked at the players I had, and decided I'd try to use for England the system that I had invented at Ipswich, and which took them to the First Division title. That's a well-documented story, players like inside-left Jimmy Leadbetter operating as a wing man. He was busy, skilful and constructive. All he did was use those qualities on the flank.

England went to Spain and beat them 2–0, our first-ever victory there, and the plan was hailed as a triumph. All I did was utilise the talent I had available in the best possible way. Robson might have to do the same. Players he has already made a mental note to discard may get a second chance. You are always looking to improve. If there is nobody better, use what you've got in the best way you can. It has surprised me how Robson took so long to contact me and ask my advice about Mexico. Three times he said he'd love to meet up for a chat, three times he couldn't make it.

Preparation is so vital. The food you eat, the water, the problem of boredom, illness – it's vital to get it all right. England would never have won the World Cup in Mexico in 1970, even had we beaten Brazil in Guadalajara and not lost 3–2 to West Germany in that killer quarter-final. The Brazilians were always going to be that much fitter, stronger and more adaptable to the altitude and heat. Believe me, the conditions can be a killer. That's why no European side has won the World Cup in South America. Bobby Charlton, for instance, would lose 9lbs a match. Players had to fill themselves with water even at the risk of being physically sick. And after a game you couldn't satisfy their thirst. The dangers of dehydration are very real.

Boredom will be a problem for Robson to overcome. In 1970 it was too hot to sunbathe by the pool, or even leave the hotel. That's something he must organise. The Mexicans burned all our meat on arrival, saying their food was good enough. But you had to be really careful about salads and fresh fruit – the foods players will want in high temperatures and heat. It says much for our thoroughness that only one player was ill, goalkeeper Gordon Banks.

Robson must get it right. Food, drink, medical facilities and organisation for the players that will make the time pass more comfortably.

We almost succeeded in 1970. There's no reason why England, 16 years on, can't do the same.

MY ENGLAND TEAM

BRIAN CLOUGH

Brian Clough comes up (naturally) with a controversial thought or two as he reveals the squad he would select for Mexico.

Who would I pick for the World Cup? Well, I think Bobby Robson has assembled just about the best squad he could for the tournament but I don't go along with his thinking in one vital area – the strikers.

Everybody is wondering whether Mark Hateley or Kerry Dixon will get the striker's place in the eventual England side but as far as I'm concerned this isn't the kind of tournament for either of them. I don't think it will be an old-fashioned England centre-forward's type of World Cup, even though I appreciate that many foreign defences are a bit scared of anybody who is brave in the air. I am sure there will be matches coming up in Mexico where that bravery factor could win us the game but I feel very strongly that it is going to be the nippy, skilful types who are going to produce the goals under the conditions out there.

For my money, Gary Lineker would be an absolute certainty. Even a change of clubs this season has done his goalscoring powers no harm at all. He has kept on scoring for Everton just as he did with Leicester. Usually, you find there is a reaction when a player like that changes clubs for a lot of money and it says plenty for his temperament that his scoring momentum has not been disrupted. Lineker, for me, has all the attributes of a top-class striker. Also, I'd definitely take Peter Davenport. I know that until recently he was one of my players at Forest and that I am probably biased but he would be ideal for Mexico with his close control skills. Mind you, Bobby Robson might have to send him back home to Birkenhead every weekend just to keep him happy!

There are a few clever players around like Davenport at the moment and the ones I also admire are Gary Bannister of Queen's Park Rangers and Peter Beardsley of Newcastle. I tried to sign Bannister before he went to

QPR because of his ability, just like Lineker, to score for anybody. With QPR he has kept on knocking them in, just as he did at Sheffield Wednesday. His style is tailor-made for that plastic pitch at Loftus Road, and he has the sort of sharpness that England will need to break down defences. As for Beardsley, when we beat Newcastle last season he was, for 15 minutes, the most outstanding striker I had seen for a long time, pure world class. And from what I have heard this season he has been producing that kind of form regularly, and it got him a deserved chance in the game against Egypt in January. Anyway, if Beardsley doesn't frighten the opposition with his skill he could always scare them by taking his teeth out.

Liverpool's little Paul Walsh is another I'd take with me, because at that level of competition you must go with who you know and who you can trust. With Kenny Dalglish unfit or unwilling to pick himself this season, Walsh has come more and more into his own, settled his differences with the club and started doing the business like he used to at Luton. So, for me, Walsh is a 'trustie'. If you hope to win any major competition you don't take kids along. Kids have a habit of letting you down, no matter how much potential they show, and if you're going for a prize like this you've got to know who's battling for you.

Somebody who gave me value for money at Forest was Peter Shilton. I have been saying for years that Shilton is not only the best in England but the best in the world, and I still can't see anybody to touch him.

When we were winning championships and cups at Forest, Shilton wasn't exactly overworked, but we always knew that when he *was* needed

World Cup qualifiers: England's three-goal hero Gary Lineker is pursued by Turkey's Ismail Demirez

Skill on the ball from Peter Davenport, now with Manchester Utd.

he would produce it. That's the kind of feeling you want on your side if you are attempting to win something as big as the World Cup. Shilts will spread confidence, not only through the back four but throughout the entire side.

I haven't seen that much of Gary Bailey and Chris Woods recently but I know enough about them to be certain England will have no problems in the goalkeeping department. When Woods was with us at Forest I was aware I had a goalkeeper of exceptional talent, as he showed in the League Cup final of 1978 (and the replay) against Liverpool. I would dearly like to have kept him but he became impatient for regular first-team football and there was no way at that time he could have replaced Shilton. When you've got the world's best it is foolish not to use him. But Woods's progress has not surprised me one bit. He does, as yet, have to prove himself at international level, but he certainly has the ability to do it.

When you sum it up, goalkeeper is the one position where we can take on the world and know there aren't many serious challengers. If we were as good as this in all positions as we are in goal we would walk the World Cup.

For the reasons I mentioned earlier, I would pack the back four with experience. At full-back I can't think of anybody better than Gary Stevens and Kenny Sansom. I would take Viv Anderson too, and I also rate Gary Mabbutt as a utility player, especially as cover for left-back. When we played Tottenham, if I had been their manager, I would have stuck Mabbutt up front because wherever he plays he has an enthusiasm that rubs off. There have been a few times this season when Tottenham have been in need of a boost and he's the all-purpose type of player who's essential.

As for Stevens, he impresses me as the best full-back to emerge for a long, long time. He seems to have everything – an excellent all-round footballer. I first noticed him before Everton came to prominence and I thought at the time Howard Kendall had got himself a performer of special talent.

The key men at the heart of the defence will be Terry Butcher and Alvin Martin. Butcher, again, would go purely on experience. He has held Ipswich up in the First Division for some time now and has been around the England scene long enough to be relied on. I always remember Bobby Robson telling me when he was Ipswich manager that you could bet your mortgage on 'Butch'. Never mind those young men knocking in the goals for West Ham, Martin is one of the big reasons for the club's success this season. He's the best centre-half in the League at the moment and that's not only my opinion. When I chat to my son Nigel about the players he is up against he has told me the same thing. That counts for more than anything because you don't get a better opinion about anyone than when you are up against them.

There is one regret I have about the make-up of England's defence. Twelve months ago I would certainly have bet on another of my players, Chris Fairclough, to win a place in the squad because he had shown me he was one of the top young defenders in the game. He carried us last season as a 19-year-old and with even a reasonable amount of progress he was ready to become an outstanding player. Then came that worrying groin injury

A man for all reasons: Gary Mabbutt, Tottenham's capable utility player

A moment of fierce concentration against Turkey for Terry Butcher
Time and Clough on his side: Chris Fairclough of Nottingham Forest

Part of West Ham's success – Alvin Martin

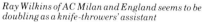

Ray Wilkins of AC Milan and England seems to be doubling as a knife-throwers' assistant

The outstanding Peter Reid of Everton

and the operation and at the time of writing he still hadn't kicked a ball for us this season. But he has lots of time on his side.

In midfield, a hell of a lot depends on Bryan Robson's fitness because of his inspirational qualities as a captain and a performer. He adapts himself so brilliantly to the circumstances. When you have to battle he rolls up his sleeves and if there is time to plonk it around he can do that, too. And, as he has often showed for both Manchester United and England, he can also come up with that priceless commodity, goals. I'm afraid I have to put a question mark alongside the name of Glenn Hoddle. There is no doubt that if he applied himself in Mexico there would be few more gifted players in the World Cup. Some of the things he is capable of would make us go into raptures if we saw them from a Brazilian or a Frenchman. I have always been a big fan of his ability but there has always been this nagging doubt about his fitness, and that bothers me. When the heat is on, as it will be in every sense of the word in Mexico, you need players to go out carrying knocks and bruises and not show it as they get on with the job.

Ray Wilkins is a midfielder who never numbered me among his biggest fans. I have always thought he played too square and too much within his own strengths to be really effective, but over the years he does seem to have developed into a better player and seems to be a good sort to have around. Without knowing Ray I would imagine him to be a useful member of a squad when it comes to geeing other people up.

Twelve months ago I would not have had a second's hesitation in taking

Trevor Steven (Everton) going wide for goal

Watch out Brazil, here comes John Barnes of England

Peter Reid. He was absolutely outstanding in Everton's championship run but, of course, has had severe injury problems since then. It was good to see him back in February after two Achilles tendon operations but, if there is some remaining doubt about his match fitness and stamina when the time comes to nominate the squad, I could think of no better option as a replacement than his team-mate Paul Bracewell. He hasn't got Hoddle's flair or Robson's all-round ability but he does possess the kind of dependable talent that's so useful. Another Everton midfielder, Trevor Steven, shouldn't be left behind either. He's a very functional player, gives you width – and also gives you goals.

I was pleased to see Gordon Cowans making an international comeback in Egypt. I tried to buy him when he was at Aston Villa, but he chose to stay with them. At that time there wasn't a better midfield player in the country. He used to make things happen. I am not sure what he has been doing in Italy, apart from getting himself injured for a long spell, but if his call-up for England in January is an indication that he has come back to anything like his best then he must be considered for Mexico.

Finally, wingers. I would definitely take John Barnes. He has shone already on the international stage and clearly has the skill required at world level. But I'm not so sure about Chris Waddle, though. He obviously has a lot of talent but from what I have seen of him, particularly this season, he has not imposed himself in the manner that you would want of an international. If I was picking one of these two it would have to be Barnes.

MEXICO '86:
THE STADIA AND THE CITIES

SIMON INGLIS

Where they play can be just as important as who and what. Simon Inglis, author of the acclaimed Football Grounds of England and Wales, *looks at the stadia where this tournament's games will take place.*

Every four years the Olympics provide a wonderful excuse for host nations to indulge in what one critic described as 'structural exhibitionism'. The Coliseum in Los Angeles was a triumph of scale and pseudo-classical pomp. Munich's Olympic Stadium broke our preconceptions about stadium design with its sweeping, translucent roofs.

But World Cups are different; they inspire little new architecture of note. The national football stadium is dusted down or an Olympic stadium borrowed, while club grounds are enlarged or temporarily modified for those few, intense weeks during which previously unknown venues like Ayresome Park, Middlesbrough, and La Rosaleda Stadium, Malaga, suddenly become the focus of worldwide attention.

Prestige stadiums are expensive. Before the 1982 World Cup in Spain, for example, approximately £45 million, nearly three-quarters of the competition's total cost, was spent on reconstructing 17 stadiums in 14 different cities.

Mexico too has had to undertake a large programme of building for the 1986 finals. In 1970, when only 16 teams competed, Mexico prepared five stadiums in five different cities. In 1986, with 24 teams involved, a total of twelve stadiums in nine cities will be used.

The northernmost are the Estadios Tecnológico and Universitario, both in the industrial city of Monterrey. England, unluckily for them, are drawn to play here, along with Poland, Morocco and Portugal. Dubbed 'the Pittsburgh of Mexico' because of the city's high output of iron and steel, Monterrey is Mexico's third largest city. It boasts the best brewery, is fond of bullfighting and, because of its proximity to the US border, baseball. But in World Cup terms it is the short straw; too low and too hot.

Neither football stadium is of architectural note. The main venue is the Estadio Universitario, an open bowl, capacity 44,000, where the Mexican

League side Monterrey play their home games. The Estadio Tecnológico is less developed and seats 34,000.

Several hundred miles of desert and semi-arid land separate Monterrey from a group of three World Cup venues around the more fertile and greener regions of the Bajio, the granary of central Mexico.

In the small city of León, 225 miles northwest of Mexico City, is the Nuevo Campo stadium, which in 1970 was host to matches in Group Four. The altitude is 6,186 feet. Together with Irapuato, it will be the venue for Group C matches involving France, Canada, Hungary and the Soviet Union.

In common with all stadiums built in Mexico in the last 25 years, the Nuevo Campo is built on the quadric plan, whereby the stands, rather than being built parallel to the touchlines, arc curved slightly. This cuts out the stretching and straining to which most British fans are accustomed whenever the ball is in the opposite corner on the nearside of the pitch.

Opened officially on 1 February 1967 with an exhibition match between Santos and River Plate, the Nuevo Campo is the home of a minor club, Curtidores, and the better known León.

In the 1970 finals León was the smallest venue, with a capacity of 25,300. Since then it has been enlarged to 31,336 by raising the banks of uncovered seating on three sides. The stadium's most unusual feature is the east side, where the seats are completely overshadowed by a tall, curving wall of private boxes on three tiers. Each tier is lined by advertisements and dotted with spectators, shaded by a 66-foot cantilevered roof.

The sun-baked concrete stands opposite and on either side, backed by trees and green foliage, are in complete contrast to this cool, imposing structure. Despite its memories for English fans after the 3–2 defeat by West Germany in the 1970 quarter-finals, León is one of Mexico's most popular settings. The city itself, roughly the size of Bradford, is best known for its shoes and intricate leatherwork.

Sixty miles south and linked with León for Group C matches is the Estadio Revolucion (capacity 40,000) in Irapuato, a small farming town which, were it not for the Irapuato football club, would be completely unknown.

Monterrey's Stadio Universitario, the larger of the Group F stadia

The Stadio Tecnológico in Monterrey where England play their first game, against Portugal, on 3 June

Still in the Bajio region, 70 miles due east of Irapuato is Querétaro, a historic small city with an unrivalled place in Mexico's turbulent revolutionary past. Here Scotland will be based, with West Germany, Uruguay and Denmark. The Corregidora Stadium, capacity 39,000, was opened in February 1985 with a tournament played between Switzerland, Bulgaria and Poland. It derives its name from a nineteenth-century war heroine.

It is linked for Group E matches with the Estadio Neza, capacity 35,000, in Nezahualcoyotl, a depressing shanty-town on the edges of Mexico City. The stadium was originally named after the Mexican president José Lopez Portilla at its inauguration in August 1982, but since his departure from office and decline in popularity the name has been dropped.

West of the Bajio region and 365 miles northwest of Mexico City is the country's second largest city, Guadalajara, which shares with the capital and Puebla the largest share of matches in the 1986 finals, and will be the starting-off point for Brazil, Northern Ireland, Spain and Algeria.

There are two stadiums in Guadalajara. The little known Estadio 3 de Marzo, with a capacity of 30,015, will be used for three Group D matches. An open but pleasant stadium, its main feature is a sloping pitch. The more famous Estadio Jalisco will stage matches up to and including one semi-final.

Guadalajara, 5,415 feet above sea level, has an almost perfect climate, much beloved among elderly Americans. It is also a football stronghold, with two major teams rivalling each other for honours.

The Jalisco stadium, situated opposite the city's main bullring, was officially opened on 31 January 1960 with a match between local club Atlas and Almogro of Argentina. Three clubs, two top level and one lesser, share the stadium: Atlas, Guadalajara and Oro.

Since its inauguration the Jalisco Stadium (named after the state of Jalisco) has been reconstructed twice. For the 1970 World Cup, when England were given such a hostile welcome at the stadium in their opening match, three tiers of boxes were installed all around the upper level of seating. As at León, a cantilevered roof covered one side, creating awkward shadows across half the pitch. This and the uneven, richly-turfed surface provoked complaints from the then England manager Alf Ramsey.

Since 1970 the stadium has undergone further changes and with its unbroken roof covering the bowl it now resembles a smaller version of the Aztec Stadium in Mexico City, its capacity totalling 66,193.

The venue furthest south is Puebla, which in 1970 shared the matches of Group Two and now shares those of Italy, Argentina, South Korea and Bulgaria in Group A. A distance of 84 miles southeast of Mexico City, Puebla is an old Spanish colonial city which in recent years has been marred by earthquake damage and a rapid growth in both industry and population (it is roughly the size of Leeds).

The Estadio Cuauhtémoc, the newest venue used in 1970, was opened on 6 October 1968 with a match between Mexico and Czechoslovakia. It

Not to Sir Alf's liking but reconstructed since then: the Jalisco Stadium at Guadalajara

follows the same quadric plan as at León and Guadalajara and has the same 75 x 115 yard pitch, yet because the overall turf area is larger spectators at Puebla are slightly further from the touchline. Enlarged since 1970 to hold 46,416, the Estadio Cuauhtémoc is neat but apparently without any focal point apart from a roof over the west side.

There is one other venue outside Mexico City, and Toluca, 40 miles west of the capital, where Mexico, Belgium, Paraguay and Iraq will be based, is undoubtedly the most unusual. Firstly, it is the most old-fashioned, having been opened on 8 August 1954 with a match between Toluca and Dynamo of Yugoslavia. Secondly, it is officially called the Luis Gutierrez Dosal Stadium, but everyone knows it as 'La Bombonera' or Chocolate Box. (Such a nickname probably refers to a box-like stand formerly at the ground. The name was possibly borrowed from Boca Juniors of Argentina. Southampton's ground, The Dell, also had a trio of stands called the Chocolate Boxes.)

Thirdly, in appearance Toluca's stadium resembles a typically English Second or Third Division ground. The three covered stands are of different designs, rectangular and close to the touchline. There is even an uncovered terrace at the west end with room for 7,800 spectators, a feature found at no other Mexican World Cup venue. In 1970 Toluca shared the Group Two matches with Puebla, but attendances were the lowest, with two gates of under 10,000. The current capacity is 32,612.

Familiar though Toluca may seem architecturally, La Bombonera has three natural disadvantages. It is the highest of the 12 stadiums, with an altitude of 8,712 feet. Heavy rainfall makes for a heavy surface, and because the pitch is built on an east-west axis the sun can be a considerable problem. Toluca kick off their League matches at 11.30am, thus avoiding the glare but catching the sun at its hottest.

Finally, there are two venues in the capital, Mexico City. The smaller of the two, on the southwestern outskirts, is variously referred to as University '68, Mexico '68, University City Stadium or the Olympic Stadium. Suffice it to say that it was the centrepiece for the 1968 Olympic Games. Originally built in 1952 the stadium was completely renovated for the Olympics and is now the home of one of Mexico's top football clubs, UNAM. Its design and history are worth noting briefly. The area on which the stadium is built is called the Pedregal, a large, uneven expanse of ancient and dark volcanic rock which is separated from the rest of Mexico City by rows of trees. The black rock dominates the entire university campus, like lumps of coal embedded into an otherwise leafy garden.

Tons of these rocks were dug up to create the saddle-like shape of the stadium, with its rising and falling banks of seating around an oval field and track. Tunnels leading to the seats were literally cut into the volcanic rock. The stadium is quite stunning. Completely exposed to the sun, it is overlooked by Las Calderas mountains and the distant ridges of extinct volcanoes. The design was by Augusto Perez Palacios, and in plan is an oval placed within a circle. Around the external sloping banks are huge polychrome murals by Diego Rivera; these stand out strongly against the bleached concrete walls and paths, and truly reflect the mood of modern Mexican architecture with its sympathetic leanings towards pre-Colonial art forms.

The University '68 stadium is the only World Cup venue with a running track between spectators and the pitch, but it is at least a famous track – the first synthetic all-weather surface ever used for an Olympic Games.

Those Games were of course marred by the massacre of Mexican students on the adjacent campus. These killings brought home to many that however contented Mexico appears at first sight – its people gentle, its arts and culture thriving – the one-party rule of the PRI can at times be as dictatorial as any in Latin America. The University '68 saw blood again in 1985, when eight football supporters died in a crush before a title match between local rivals America and UNAM. A crowd of 80,000 had tried to squeeze through those volcanic tunnels. The stadium only holds 72,200.

The Aztec Stadium, which will stage nine World Cup matches including the opening event and the final, is Mexico's pride and joy, hardly surprising when one takes into account the nation's relatively poor standing in world football. But then Latin America is full of excellent stadiums in the most obscure of places.

Designed by Pedro R. Vasquez, an architect who was also chairman of the Organising Committee for the 1968 Olympic Games, the Aztec Stadium was first conceived in the early 1960s. At that time, apart from the 1952

'Like the wheel rim of a motor car on a mudflat' – the 115,000-seater Aztec Stadium where Italy and Bulgaria kick off the championship

University Stadium, Mexico's main venue was the rather dull National Stadium, built in 1923 (the same year as Wembley).

Vasquez, an award-winning architect mainly known for overseeing the construction of some 35,000 schools in Mexico, was determined that any structure put up for the Olympics should be of lasting value to the country, and so he made visits to eight other major cities to study their stadiums.

As early as 1962 it was clear that private boxes were going to be desirable assets (England's first boxes were at Old Trafford in 1965) and that road access to certain parts of the stadium was vital. The budget was tight. There would be no cash for structural fantasies, and all non-essential features and decorations would be rejected.

The final design took four years to execute, under the direction of Rafael Mijares Alcerra. Built on flat scrubland beyond the southeast outskirts of the city, the Aztec Stadium rose like the wheel rim of a motor car on a mudflat. It cost £7 million, took seven million man hours to build, and required 100,000 tons of concrete (four times the amount used to build Wembley). And although the result was hardly inspirational from an aesthetic point of view, at the time it was probably the most advanced football stadium in the world. Opened on 26 May 1966 with a match between Mexico and Torino (seven weeks before the World Cup finals began in London), it held 107,494 spectators, all seated. The first major international matches were those in the 1968 Olympic Games – though the stadium itself was not built with Olympic funds. The Aztec played a central role in the 1970 World Cup finals and, true to Vasquez's intentions, has been in twice-weekly use ever since.

Four of Mexico City's major clubs – America, Atlante, Necaxa and Cruz Azul – have played the majority of their home games there since 1966 (although Atlante recently moved to another stadium because the Aztec's rent was too high).

Since 1970 major renovation work has been completed at the stadium, smartening up its rather utilitarian aspect and increasing the capacity to 115,000. There are 577 private boxes on three levels. These divide the lower tier of seating from the upper two tiers. A continuous cantilevered roof, 150 feet in span, covers approximately 80 per cent of the seats.

Box owners, who originally paid only £5,000 for their 99-year leases (each box holds ten people), have their own drive-in access to the stadium, and together with the teams and other dignitaries they can actually park underneath the stands.

In fact the Azteca somewhat resembles a huge multi-storey car park from the outside. In addition, there are vast open spaces around the stadium, with room for approximately 17,000 cars, and, it would sometimes appear, the same number of food and souvenir vendors. A tube station links the stadium with the city centre and there is a motorway 200 yards from the stadium's main entrance. English fans accustomed to battling their way through Wembley's tortuous approaches might weep with envy.

But is the Aztec a good venue for watching football? Certainly it is tailor-made. Despite the apparently vast scale, each goal and touchline is relatively near – about 30 feet – to the lower tier of seating. The quadric plan and cantilevered roof also ensure an unencumbered view from every part of the stadium. (The stands are actually curved in a chord of three metres in a 200-metre arc, a formula first used by the ancient Greeks.)

Only from each corner of the upper tier is the viewing distance slightly longer than the optimum, the furthest point being approximately 115 yards from the centre circle. The uppermost row, however, is not so high – 150 feet above pitch level – for the action to seem too distant.

With a full, noisy house the Aztec Stadium is very special. The sky – smog conditions permitting – appears as a perfect blue oval above the lush turf (laid under the supervision of English experts), and the thin lines of advertisements encircling the seats tie the whole structure together in pleasing unity. It is spectacular theatre-in-the-round, with the fanatical Mexicans as much part of the pageant as the players themselves.

Mexico may not be the natural location for World Cup finals it is true; venues like Monterrey and Toluca are beset with disadvantages for players of any ilk, and the problems of heat and altitude exist in varying degrees at every stadium. But in terms of their design and concept the majority of Mexico's stadiums are far superior to most of those in which Britain parades its national sport. The Mexicans have every right to feel proud of their football grounds.

YOUR MEXICO '86 FORM GUIDE

The lowdown on the form, fitness and probable fortune of every contender.

ALGERIA

Past appearances: 1
Record:
P 3 **W** 2 **D** 0 **L** 1 **F** 5 **A** 5

Sprung one of the great surprises in Spain '82 when they beat West Germany in the opening round, but the cynical pact between Austria and West Germany in Gijon put paid to further progress. Their star player is 25-year-old Lakhdar Belloumi, who likes to hover behind the two main strikers and is regarded in Africa as a cross between Platini, Maradona and God. Algeria are a super little team when they attack but are catching some incredibly boring defensive habits from Europe and South America.

Spain '82: A shock for West Germany as Madjer of Algeria gazes at goal number one

ARGENTINA

Past appearances: 8
Record:
P 34 **W** 16 **D** 5 **L** 13 **F** 63 **A** 50

Do the '78 winners still depend too much on Diego Maradona? His fitness has lately been in doubt after some cracking performances during the qualifying rounds. And has the marvellous Daniel Passarella, once described by a South American journalist as 'the dirtiest great player in the world,' been able to patch up his personal differences with national manager Carlos Bilardo? Whatever their problems, Argentina are still tipped to do well in Mexico but whether they'll end up as bride rather than bridesmaid is another matter.

Diego Maradona (Argentina) takes a breather

Spain '82: Frankie Vercauteren (Belgium) and Zbigniew Boniek compete for possession

BELGIUM

Past appearances: 6
Record:
P 14   **W** 3   **D** 2   **L** 9   **F** 15   **A** 30

The bribe scandal at Standard Liege is not yet forgotten, but the recall of Eric Gerets, one of the miscreants, to the national side suggests that forgiveness is a beautiful thing. Belgium are a well-organised team who have a much better chance in Mexico than that promised by their rather dull reputation. Anderlecht's Frankie Vercauteren is an intelligent and creative midfielder and great things are being spoken of 20-year-old Enzo Scifo, i.e. 'he's the new Johan Cruyff.'

BRAZIL

Past appearances: 12
Record:
P 57   **W** 37   **D** 10   **L** 10   **F** 134   **A** 62

The reappointment of Tele Santana as manager must have brought sighs of relief to Brazil buffs who feared that the nation of Pele, Gerson and Rivelino was going to career into Mexico '86 without anyone at the steering wheel. Now the big question is who Santana deploys – the old but gifted retainers of Spain '82 (Zico, Socrates, Eder, Falcao et al) or young bloods like Walter Casagrande – and whether he can incorporate the talents of Italian expatriates Junior, Edinho and Cerezo. Brazil are among the betting favourites but some think that's just nostalgia. (See page 41.)

BULGARIA

Past appearances: 4
Record:
P 12   **W** 4   **D** 0   **L** 8   **F** 9   **A** 29

Bulgaria reached a nadir a couple of years back when their top two clubs, CSKA and Levski Spartak, the Liverpool and Manchester United of their game, were disbanded after their Cup final ended in mutual mayhem and GBH. Among those players banned for life were three internationals, including their goalie. Newly-cleansed, it's going to be interesting to see what Bulgaria come up with; they've got a reputation for excruciating dullness, but this time they could surprise us. After all, they did beat France in the qualifiers.

Irresistible Platini: But France lose 2–0 to Bulgaria in Sofia

CANADA

Past appearances: None

They're obviously going to be honorary Brits, since they are managed by Lancastrian Tony Waiters, once of Blackpool FC, now a North American hero. Waiters is a tough, articulate man who will probably get the Most Intelligent Press Conference award, even if his team hits the wall in the first round. His underdog squad features several unemployed players, and financial pressures are a continuing problem, so much so that they've undertaken a gruelling series of matches to underwrite their trip. But this will be their chance to establish soccer in Canada and they deserve your support. Players to watch include Carl Valentine of West Bromwich Albion, and Dale Mitchell. (See page 47).

DENMARK

Past appearances: None

Hard to believe that this will be Denmark's first World Cup – their rousing, surging style seems to have been a fixture in Europe for decades. Like Canada, they will probably be accorded honorary British status – if twinkle-toed giant Jan Molby and fiery midget Jesper Olsen make the team. But it's not only Denmark's English connection which excites – watch out, too, for Morten Olsen, Michael Laudrup, Soren Lerby and Preben Elkjaer. Big question – will their greased lightning game melt in the heat?

Preben Elkjaer of Denmark looking more like a Rugby League player

ENGLAND

Past appearances: 7
Record:
P 29 **W** 13 **D** 8 **L** 8 **F** 40 **A** 29

One of the finest England teams ever – Moore, Peters, Ball, Bobby Charlton and company – found the Mexican experience too much for them in 1970; do the new generation even equal them in skill and endurance? They need Bryan Robson at his fittest and paciest, Glenn Hoddle at his classiest and most involved, and one of the claimants for the chief goalscoring role (Lineker, maybe, or Hateley) to hit form at the crucial moment, and then England might just go for it. (See page 51.)

FRANCE

Past appearances: 8
Record:
P 27 **W** 11 **D** 3 **L** 13 **F** 59 **A** 50

In 1984, France were the outstanding team in Europe – two years later the midfield (Platini, Fernandez, Tigana and Giresse) are still unsurpassed. Francophobes will point out, however, that the back four has lately been unsettled – who plays sweeper, Bossis or Battiston? – and that the Blues have had trouble finding the right pairing up front. If Rocheteau and Touré prove to be made for each other, though, then France could challenge Italy as Europe's best bet for glory. (See page 57.)

HUNGARY

Past appearances: 8
Record:
P 29   **W** 14   **D** 3   **L** 12   **F** 85   **A** 48

Their dominating player is still Tibor Nyilasi, an outstanding international star for ten years who has clearly happened on Pat Jennings's cache of endless youth elixir. 'Tibi' runs the Magyars' midfield and has a shot like a Sam 7 as well. This time he's better supported by his team-mates who by the lean-honed look of them have been a bit more punctilious about their press-ups than in the past. New coach Mezey has led them to beat West Germany among others.

Still one of the world's greats: 'Tibi' Nyilasi of Hungary

IRAQ

Past appearances: None

Coached by Brazilian Jorge Keira, who took charge of the squad after they flunked the '84 Olympics. Iraq are an attacking side with a simple, short-passing game suited to their outstanding player, striker Ali Hussein. Middle Eastern football has improved noticeably in recent years but no one's claiming Iraq are going to be the big surprise of the finals.

Ali Hussein Alawa (Iraq) ponders the pros and cons of being a star striker

ITALY

Past appearances: 10
Record:
P 43   **W** 24   **D** 9   **L** 10   **F** 74   **A** 46

Paolo Rossi, whose scoring touch helped Italy to their triumph in '82, is back on form; there is new blood in the shape of Franco Tancredi (latest man to fill the jersey of the great Dino Zoff) and other young sprigs are challenging the likes of Bruno Conti and Marco Tardelli for a place in the team. In other words, the Cup holders are looking good. Will Enzo Bearzot crown a decade as national manager by making it two in a row? (See page 61.)

MEXICO

Past appearances: 8
Record:
P 24　**W** 3　**D** 4　**L** 17　**F** 21　**A** 62

Being hosts in 1970 appeared to give Mexico very little advantage. Even with some dodgy refereeing decisions in their favour they put up one of the most dreary acts in the entire circus. This time, though, they've limbered up for the Big One with something like four dozen matches in less than two years. Poor results in Africa and Asia notwithstanding, Mexico have a real chance to make amends and Hugo Sanchez is always a compensation.

Always a compensation: Hugo Sanchez of Mexico

'Zaki' Badou of Morocco with one of the shots that didn't get away

MOROCCO

Past appearances: 1
Record:
P 3　**W** 0　**D** 1　**L** 2　**F** 2　**A** 6

Another small side whose injections of Brazilian skill and art – Mehdi (née Jose) Favia is their coach – give them an opportunity to win friends. Their keeper, captain and star personality is Zaki, full name Badou Ezaki, who is regarded as Africa's finest. Only one shot got past him in eight games in the tough African section of the qualifiers so he'll be a great test for a few centre-forwards, including England's.

NORTHERN IRELAND

Past appearances: 2
Record:
P 10　**W** 3　**D** 4　**L** 3　**F** 11　**A** 17

Against all predictions they really made the tournament in Spain and clearly it would be silly to chunter on now about the limited size of the squad, injuries to key players, advancing decrepitude of others, etc, etc. Northern Ireland retain a marvellous capacity to delight and astonish that for some people is the reason why they continue to love football in spite of everything. Martin O'Neill will no doubt try and play even if held together by glue and old paper-clips, Pat Jennings has lost none of his gusto for the big occasion and Norman Whiteside would be an automatic inclusion in any team in the tournament. (See page 66.)

It's okay, boys, I've changed my mind: Cayetano Re, the much-resigning manager of Paraguay

PARAGUAY

Past appearances: 3
Record: P 7   W 2   D 2   L 3   F 12   A 19

Most of Paraguay's squad, like their top striker Canete Cabanas, have had to be trawled from well-paid jobs abroad (the home economy is too lousy to keep a footballer happy). What's more, their manager Cayetano Re spent much of the early run-up to the tournament promising to resign. Anyway, they've made it but understandably they're not the most desperately consistent of the South Americans and can't really be expected to make the biggest splash.

POLAND

Past appearances: 4
Record:
P 21   W 12   D 4   L 5   F 38   A 22

It's their fourth successive World Cup which is why they're among the top seeds – though informed natives reckon they're also the weakest of them, with current uncertainty in defence to add to all the problems of acclimatisation shared with England. But it would be a mistake to write off the team of Boniek and Zmuda, who's made a return to form. As well as the experienced internationals, they've got an enthusiastic clutch of rookies – the average age of the squad is 23. Must be a quarter-final bet, at the very least. (See page 71.)

PORTUGAL

Past appearances: 1
Record:
P 6   W 5   D 0   L 1   F 17   A 8

Fernando Gomes (Portugal) hurdles Harald Shumacher (West Germany) with Ditmar Jakobs

England beat them against the betting odds in 1966, and that was their last appearance. But they were the first country to defeat West Germany in the qualifiers and their attack is built round Fernando Gomes of FC Porto. Last year this phenomenal 28-year-old won the Adidas Golden Boot award again with 39 goals in 30 games. He has also scored 16 times in internationals and makes Gary Lineker look like a slouch.

SCOTLAND

Past appearances: 5
Record:
P 14 **W** 3 **D** 5 **L** 6 **F** 20 **A** 29

No one will be able to accuse Scotland of arriving in Mexico by hot-air balloon. The swagger of Argentina '78 has been replaced by caution and humility; they've got a fairly desperate draw after all. But don't discount them – for the first time in years they have a genuine class goalie in Jim Leighton, they are led by the magnificent Graeme Souness, and if Frank McAvennie does for them what he's managed to achieve for West Ham then all need not be lost. (See page 76.)

SOUTH KOREA

Past appearances: 1
Record:
P 2 **W** 0 **D** 0 **L** 2 **F** 0 **A** 16

Their record speaks for itself – two losses, sixteen goals conceded and none scored. Surprised? No, you're thinking of North Korea. In 1966 they were responsible for the Italians getting a load of tomatoes chucked over them and they also gave Portugal a giant fright. The lads from the South are disciplined and fit but very defensive. In other words, they probably won't repeat the 9-0 defeat by Hungary in 1954 but will be good news for insomniacs. (See page 81.)

SOVIET UNION

Past appearances: 5
Record:
P 24 **W** 12 **D** 5 **L** 7 **F** 37 **A** 25

Prognoses of the Soviets' chances in Mexico have improved since Oleg Blokhin, their blond super-winger, has had a career revival. They did well in 1970, so obviously know how to cope with the conditions, have a terrific goalie in Rinat Dasayev and are nicely organised in attack. But will they flatter only to deceive as they did in Spain in 1982? (See page 84.)

SPAIN

Past appearances: 6
Record:
P 23 **W** 8 **D** 5 **L** 10 **F** 26 **A** 30

Hipolito Rincon: one of Spain's new stars

Spain have built up a reputation for being one of the least lovable teams in Europe, with tackling that varies from the hairy-chested to the positively homicidal. However, they did do well in the European Championships and, if they can curb their more macho propensities, then new players like the wonderfully-named Hipolito Rincon should show that they can also attack with brio and intelligence.

URUGUAY

Past appearances: 10
Record:
P 29 **W** 14 **D** 5 **L** 10 **F** 57 **A** 39

They're the South American champions and by rights ought to have been given a slot among the top seeds – after all, look at their record in the World Cup itself. However, unlike their flashier cousins in Brazil, their players are hardly household names in Great Britain – how much have you heard recently about the talented Venancio Ramos? Coach Omar Borras also has the bother of dragging his squad back from various points of the compass where they've scattered in pursuit of loot. But they've got what it takes. They could even go all the way.

WEST GERMANY

Past appearances: 10
Record:
P 54 **W** 31 **D** 11 **L** 12 **F** 122 **A** 78

Franz Beckenbauer, now national coach, has spent so much time publicly writing off his team that you've got to suspect him of gamesmanship. In actual fact, this is potentially a strong squad and Beckenbauer's goading will no doubt extract world-class performances – not only from old favourite Karl-Heinz Rummenigge. Mathias Herget adds new quality and much good is spoken of youngster Olaf Thon – will he become one of the bright stars of the finals? Harald Schumacher, who perpetrated that terrible foul on Patrick Battiston in Spain, is still unrepentant keeping goal. (See page 88.)

Not yet a household name, but Venancio Ramos of Uruguay could set everyone talking in Mexico

THE MAGIC OF BRAZILIAN FOOTBALL

KEIR RADNEDGE

The magic of Brazilian football is legend for all those supporters the world over who have marvelled – live or on television – at these South American masters. Keir Radnedge of World Soccer Magazine reminds us of past heroes and gives an update on the new stars.

No Who's Who of the world game could ever be complete without generous reference to the stars who made possible the first-ever World Cup hat-trick in 1958 (in Sweden), in 1962 (in Chile) and in 1970 (in Mexico).

Paramount among those heroes will always be the great Pele who, at 17, scored twice in the 5–2 victory over Sweden in the Stockholm final of 1958. But for more than a decade he drew inspired support from the likes of goalkeeper Gilmar, full-backs Djalma and Nilton Santos, Zito and Didi and later Gerson and Rivelino in midfield, and, in attack, Garrincha, Vava, Mario Zagalo, Jairzinho and Tostao.

It's no wonder that Brazil have a wonderful World Cup record; they are the only nation to have been ever-present in the finals since the game's premier event was launched in 1930. It's little wonder either that, over the years, Brazil's players have been leading targets for the talent-hunters of the rich Italian and Spanish clubs.

Brazil are the most powerful football nation on earth. Their World Cup achievements, their apparently endless conveyor belt of new talent – Brazil have won the last two World Youth Cups – plus the fact that the president of FIFA, Joao Havelange, is Brazilian, surely prove the point.

Teams and countries in such positions often inspire envious criticism. Not Brazil. The reason lies in the nature of the Brazilian footballer: he is not a robotic player but an explosive entertainer, gifted with a technical ability superior to that found in any other country, even in South America.

That exuberance can be counter-productive. Against Italy in the 1982 World Cup in Barcelona, Brazil needed only a draw to reach the semi-finals. But their players' relentless need to attack sent them driving forward time after time ... and, on three fatal occasions, the brilliant Paolo Rossi ran clear on the break to punish them with decisive goals.

The 1982 World Cup was a sadder event after Brazil went home. The rest

The magic of Pele: French goalie Abbes is beaten by him for the third time as Brazil crush France in Sweden '58

At last, a manager...Tele Santana fills a crucial gap in the Brazil line-up as the South Americans prepare for Mexico

of the game acclaimed them in defeat. But back home the fans were not happy. The *torcida* expect nothing less than total success. Other countries would have celebrated finishing fourth in the World Cup (as Brazil did in 1974) or third (as in 1978). But such was the domestic disappointment that each time the manager paid with his job: Mario Zagalo in 1974; Claudio Coutinho in 1978. And in 1982 Tele Santana was only too happy after the World Cup to take up a lucrative contract in Saudi Arabia.

High standards indeed. But then, that had been the way with Brazilian football ever since one Charles Miller sailed home to Sao Paulo from Britain in the 1890s to introduce the game. A league began in Sao Paulo in 1902 and another in Rio de Janeiro four years later. Indeed, one of the greatest clubs took its name from the legendary British team, the Corinthians.

The Brazilian sports confederation was set up in 1914 and a year later Brazil joined FIFA. In 1919 they won the South American championship for the first time – the winning goal scored by their first great player, Arthur Friedenreich. He would not only run up a career world record of 1,329 goals but was also the first coloured player to break down racial barriers in what had previously been mainly a middle-class sport.

Once the breakthrough had been established, football quickly became the passport to fame and fortune for any poor kid who was good enough. Many stars began playing for fun on the beaches of Copacabana and Ipanaema ... and ended up as virtual gods.

In the thirties, full-back Domingos da Guia and the original Black Diamond centre-forward, Leonidas da Silva, were two such heroes. In the 1950 World Cup Brazil finished runners-up on home ground in the vast Maracana stadium in Rio thanks to a brilliant inside-forward trio made up of Zizinho, Ademir and Jair. Then along came Pele and Co.

Brazilians demand much of their players. Most clubs play around 70 first-class games a year and players are quickly burned out. The secret of Brazil's success is that, in the past at least, there have always been more talented youngsters clamouring to fill their places.

But a question mark has now been placed against the continuance of that tradition. In both Rio and Sao Paulo crowds are well down, except for the few decisive play-off derbies. Zico, Brazil's No. 1 player for the past decade, blames too much violence; Santana, the most respected coach and the man who agreed finally to lead the team to Mexico, blames the bad judgement 'which turns any player who has one good pass into a superstar.'

The challenge facing Brazil's 1986 World Cup squad is not only to reassert Brazil's international superiority, but to revitalise the game at home.

The financial crisis which has affected much of the world's professional game hit Brazil too. Top clubs such as Flamengo and Fluminense of Rio, Corinthians and Sao Paulo FC, had no option but to sell their star players to Europe. World cup stars Zico, Falcao, Socrates, Edinho and Junior all moved to Italy and the national team had to be rebuilt from nothing.

Carlos Alberto Parreira, who took Kuwait to the 1982 finals, was brought home to run Brazil's team. But defeat by old rivals Uruguay in the final of the 1983 South American championship was followed by his departure. Edu, elder brother of Zico, who had been successful as coach of Vasco da Gama, took over. But his reign lasted only a handful of matches after the humiliation of defeat in Maracana by England.

Evaristo de Macedo, one-time centre-forward with Flamengo and Spain's Barcelona, was next man in the hot seat. He didn't last long either. His brief had been to guide Brazil through the World Cup qualifiers in early 1985. But Evaristo's Brazil looked as ill-at-ease as that of Edu and, on the eve of the qualifying series, he too was replaced.

Giulite Coutinho, president of the CBF, sent to Saudi Arabia for Santana. His club did not mind because their season had just ended, so Santana flew home to pick up the pieces.

Brazil's task was not a difficult one, matched as they were in a group with Bolivia and Paraguay. Santana summoned the nucleus of his 1982 squad – including the Italian-based exiles – and virtually ensured qualification in just the first two matches.

Both brought victories by 2–0, first in Bolivia, then in Paraguay. Walter Casagrande, new centre-forward hero of Corinthians Sao Paulo, scored both goals in Bolivia and one in Paraguay. Back home Brazil needed merely to avoid defeat in their next match, against the Paraguayans, to ensure their place in Mexico. The result was a 1–1 draw which disappointed the fans but at least lifted the immense pressure on Santana and his team. The final group match also ended in a 1–1 draw, at home to Bolivia. But, most important, Brazil were again through to the finals.

The confederation could not, however, start planning the Mexico campaign. Santana had gone back to fulfil his contract in Saudi Arabia, and without a manager there could be no team. Not only that, but the appointment of a manager for the Mexico trip had to be delayed until after the CBF presidential elections in January – just over four months before the start of the World Cup finals.

The good news was that Zico, Socrates and Falcao had all returned from Italy. Zico and Socrates joined Flamengo while Falcao signed for Sao Paulo and helped them win their state championship. But while Falcao did so only after almost a year sidelined by injury, both Zico and Socrates missed much of the Rio State League because of injuries.

Zico collected a knee injury after being badly fouled in a match against Bangu, while Socrates broke an ankle in training before he had even kicked a ball in anger for his new club. It was recognised, however, that these two men would shoulder much of the responsibility for Brazil's World Cup bid, fitness permitting.

Zico is now 33, the youngest of four brothers who all played First Division football. Zico was originally thought too small. But Flamengo put this skinny teenager on a body-building course; he has since rewarded that faith with around 600 goals for club, country and for the Italian side,

Zico of Brazil aims high against Argentina

Daniel Passarella wins this ball against Socrates, but victory was fleeting: Brazil finished 3–1 in front

Spain '82: the two faces of theatre as Falcao celebrates Brazil's second against Italy, Antognoni holds his head in anguish

Udinese, with whom he spent a restless two-year spell.

Zico scored with a brilliant free-kick on his Brazil debut against Uruguay in 1975 and numbers teams all round the world – including Liverpool in the 1981 World Club Cup final – among the victims of his spectacular skills.

Zico was not the only Brazilian to find mixed fortunes in Italy. He was the one star in a mediocre team at Udinese while Socrates was just one of a number of stars at the Florence club Fiorentina, but could never adapt to the change of lifestyle. A qualified doctor with a keen interest in politics, it may have been that Socrates found the life altogether too stimulating to concentrate solely on his football.

That could not be said of Falcao and fellow Brazil midfielder Toninho Cerezo – son of a circus clown – during their stay at Roma. Falcao, scorer of a most memorable goal against Italy in the 1982 World Cup, inspired Roma to their first League title in 40 years and then to the European Champions Cup final the following season.

However, defeat in front of their own fans by Liverpool meant the beginning of the end for Falcao and Roma. He missed most of the 1984-85

Leandro of Brazil shows Wynton Rufer of New Zealand how it's done in Brazil's 4–0 win in Spain '82

season because of injury, eventually underwent surgery in the United States and was transferred back to Sao Paulo during his convalescence in Brazil last summer.

A handful of Brazilian World Cup men did continue to prosper and enjoy their game in Italy, including centre-back Edinho at Udinese, and left-back or midfielder Junior at Torino. But by the start of 1986 the bulk of the World Cup probables were safely back home.

Jose Leandro at Flamengo, after domestic problems and a contract dispute, continues as one of the classiest right-backs in South America. Casagrande is a thrusting centre-forward and Eder, despite a loan-transfer to Internacional of Limeira for a season, can still hit a free-kick with all his old power.

In 1966 Brazil made the mistake of going to the World Cup finals in England with a team which relied too heavily on veterans of previous campaigns. They will not want to repeat that mistake – but whether they can successfully avoid it depends on how new youngsters such as Geovani, Bebeto or Caio Junior rise to perhaps Brazil's greatest challenge.

TONY'S BOYS STILL PLAYING FOR A DREAM

JAMES LAWTON

In a year that ravaged so much of the spirit of football, Tony Waiters was a conspicuous survivor. James Lawton, once of the Daily Express *and now Canada's top sports journalist, reports on his expatriate friend and the team Canada has built on negligible resources.*

The tall, moustachioed Lancastrian had had his moments before Canada qualified for the World Cup finals for the first time on a windblown field in St John's, Newfoundland, in September. 'I worked with Bill Shankly at Liverpool and that was a daily joy. I kept goal for England in Maracana and that was a wonderful experience for 60 minutes, after which Pele got busy and put three past me. I had some great times at Blackpool and scuffling around in management in England. But what happened in St John's, well, it was different. It was a bunch of lads, some of whom were unemployed, who were playing for a dream and by God they did it; they ran themselves silly and when it was over it was so neat I just wanted to sit down and cry.'

It was an extraordinary achievement by any standards. Waiters' team was a patchwork drawn from the torn fabric of the North American professional game. Injuries had decimated Canada at the front. Branko Segota, a Yugoslavian-born striker whose skills command $120,000 a year from the Major Indoor Soccer League club San Diego, missed the final round of qualification against Honduras and Costa Rica because Waiters didn't like his attitude. 'He came to training camp unfit and then demanded a starting position. I couldn't let the kids see this happen,' said Waiters. 'When it comes down to it you dance with the guys who got you to the ball. Branko can play – really I think he could make it in Europe – but in my position I was counting heads and hearts. In the end it paid off.'

Waiters was also without his most accomplished native-born player, Dale Mitchell, who has seen experience in the defunct North American Soccer League and is one of those rare North American players with highly developed attacking skills. Mitchell can hold the ball, shield it, buy time; a crucial asset in a game plan that demanded 90 minutes of physical pressure against more skilful Latin opponents. Another casualty before the all-important final game against Honduras was John Catliff, a blond raw-

A conspicuous survivor: Tony Waiters, Canada's man of the moment

A painful-looking clash between Ken Garraway (Canada) and Domingo Drumond (Honduras)

boned youth who developed nicely in the pressure of games in Tegucigalpa, Honduras, and San Jose, Costa Rica.

The burden of goalscoring fell to George Pakos, a 33-year-old amateur from Victoria, British Columbia, who earns his living by fixing water meters. Pakos got a big goal in Tegucigalpa, where 50,000 fans gathered in a hilltop stadium, and, somewhat unbelievably, did it again in the early minutes of the St John's game. Waiters had flown in Carl Valentine from West Bromwich, a move of dwindling value, it seemed, when the clever little winger spent much of the week in the lavatory. But Valentine rallied and played sharply for most of the game, Waiters withdrawing him in the final minutes after an acutely-placed corner had set up the winner. 'I had to bring Carl off. He was so whacked he was breathing through his bum at the end. But he was magnificent. They were all magnificent,' said Waiters.

Later the Honduran coach Jose de la Paz Herrera pecked bleakly at supper – he had written his resignation before the game – and said, 'There was no lack of commitment by my team. A lot of the players went to Spain in 1982 and they knew what was at stake today. When we tied with Spain it was a national celebration at home. None of us can look forward to going home. We could have played better, more calmly, but I have to say that Canada were extraordinary. I do not think any team in the world would have had an easy time on that field. Canada were very strong, very physical – their young forward Vrablic [Igor] scared some of my defenders. He knows how to use his strength. I have been in this game a long time. I learned to coach in Argentina. I don't remember seeing a team play as hard as Canada. They will not be disgraced in Mexico.'

Waiters was unfazed by the draw, which has Canada opening against France in León and playing Hungary and Russia in Irapuato. 'There weren't going to be any easy rides in Mexico – except maybe for Mexico – so we knew we would be in tough. How bad is it playing against France in the World Cup, being on the same field with someone like Platini? Hey, this is dream stuff.'

Despite the altitude, Canada will play in the style that carried them through Central America. 'On the ski slopes the Canadians earned the title Crazy Canucks. Well, the soccer players are going to be a bit crazy too. We know we have one chance and that's to run our asses off. We're going there ready to spill our guts,' says Bruce Wilson, the veteran left-back and skipper whose NASL career took him to Vancouver, Toronto, and New York and whose left peg is a refined instrument supported by a scuffling nature.

At 33, Wilson is aware that great players like George Best and John Giles never got to play in a World Cup; the edge of his anticipation is sharpened by the fact that for most of his career Canada's chances were reduced almost to nothing by the politics of the CONCACAF region and organisation that rarely rose above the pitiable.

He recalls that both in 1977 and 1981 Canadian teams were on the brink of striking because of the Canadian Soccer Association's refusal to negotiate bonuses. 'Back in Mexico in 1977 we were up until 2 am talking with CSA officials before a game with El Salvador. Eventually we got some kind of deal but there was a bad taste in our mouths. Everyone seemed to be considered but the players. It was the same in 1981, when we definitely should have qualified for Spain. Before flying off to Honduras we had to call a last-minute meeting and tell the officials, "no pay, no play." The great thing about Tony Waiters is that he is a pro. He knows how players tick. He knows what gets them up and what gets them down. As far as I'm concerned he arrived in the nick of time.'

In fact, Waiters, 48, had no serious rivals for the job after Barrie Clarke, an English-born schoolteacher, loaded up with coaching jargon and proceeded to make some crucial mistakes in the 1981 qualifying tournament. Clarke changed the team repeatedly, and refused to consult with senior professionals like Wilson and the team's other father figure, the boyish-faced Bobby Lenarduzzi, who grew up in the Italian quarter of East Vancouver and in his teens played for Reading in the Third Division. Clarke's final, killing gaffe was to play a college player in midfield for the pivotal game against Honduras.

'What happened in Honduras was a nightmare,' says Wilson. 'We've made some big strides since then.'

Ever since Waiters resigned as an assistant coach at Coventry City – because his fired boss Noel Cantwell was receiving only $19,000 of a

$25,000 pay-off – his strides have tended to be measured with some prudence.

In the sixties, Waiters was a rare English pro. He was a grammar school boy who got a degree at Loughborough. In eight years at Blackpool he played five times for England. After a spell on Shankly's Liverpool staff he made the romantic decision, at age 33, to return to the field and played for two years at Burnley, with mixed results. 'I ranged from adequate to bloody awful, but I'm glad I did it. I got the playing out of my system,' he says.

In North America, where he went after six years as manager of Plymouth Argyle – he got promotion to the Second Division one year and the semi-final of the League Cup another before being fired – he was appalled at the attitude of many British soccer immigrants. 'A lot of people, coaches and players, came out to con a living. It was sad. There was so much opportunity for good people to build but most of the building was on sand.'

He was among the first to see that the NASL was overambitious and underfinanced and resigned as president of the Vancouver Whitecaps in 1982 after taking the club to a Soccer Bowl triumph, a success which filled the Canadian city with thousands of celebrating fans. Waiters brought Alan Ball, Rudi Krol, Peter Lorimer and John Giles to Vancouver. He was acutely conscious that the game had to achieve high quality or it would perish in its professional form. Now in the debris of the NASL he seeks to establish a more modest Canadian Professional League, which would at least serve as a natural progression for talented young players who after high school currently face the alternatives of the Major Indoor Soccer League, a battle against heavy odds in England or Scotland, or oblivion.

'I believe that getting to Mexico is the start of a process. It is establishing in the minds of Canadians that we can produce soccer players good enough to service a professional league. In the last few years there has been a genuine explosion of young talent. There are kids coming through in Quebec, Ontario, Alberta and British Columbia who are just screaming to be taken into a competitive situation. In the summer people across the country who associate world-class competition with playing the Russians at ice hockey will see Canadian soccer players going in against the best. I think there'll be a real stirring.'

From his home overlooking a spectacular stretch of British Columbia coastline, Waiters works on coaching manuals and videos. He is defiant about the game's enduring qualities, says that it will take a firm root in North America. 'Twenty years ago you wouldn't see kids playing on a pitch in Central Park, New York. The game's established now. In the midwest the registration of players has reached amazing levels. Okay, so we had a disastrous year and maybe back in England everybody has to rethink the whole basis of how the game is marketed professionally. What happened in Brussels and Bradford was sad and disgusting but it shouldn't stop anyone believing in the game. You think of Hungary in the fifties and the Brazilians and look at this French team and you know that a game that can get so good isn't going to disappear.'

HODDLE'S LIGHT MUST SHINE IN THE MEXICO HEAT

DAVID LACEY

With England there are no half measures. Seldom do they set off for a World Cup accompanied by qualified optimism or reasonable doubt. David Lacey of the Guardian *assesses the task facing Bobby Robson and his team as they square up to their greatest challenge yet.*

Either England will carry all before them or they will fail ignominiously; the players are the best in the world or honest but inadequate triers; the manager is a man of vision or a myopic muddler.

An exception to these extremes was the last World Cup in Mexico, in 1970, when England, as holders, were able to bring logic to the argument. In Gordon Banks, Bobby Moore, Bobby Charlton, Geoff Hurst, Martin Peters and Alan Ball they had retained important elements of the 1966 triumph and these were augmented by the likes of Alan Mullery and Francis Lee.

That England team was good enough to reach the final. They were the next best side in the tournament after Brazil. But the trouble with World Cups is that once the contest has begun someone is likely to tear up the script at any given point – North Korea in 1966, Algeria in 1982.

Who could predict that England would take the crucial lead in extra time in the 1966 final on the nod of a Russian linesman or that Banks's stomach would begin to heave on the eve of the renewal of hostilities with West Germany in the quarter-finals in León four years later or that Bryan Robson would score against France in 27 seconds in Bilbao in 1982?

When considering England's prospects for Mexico in 1986 it would be unwise to judge the team wholly on its form in the qualifying competition or warm-up matches, or to pay too much heed to individual performances in the domestic competitions. Nevertheless certain evidence cannot be ignored.

Of course great players influence World Cups; Didi, Pele, Garrincha, Bobby Charlton, Tostao, Gerd Muller and Paolo Rossi have all proved that. But World Cups have also been won by good players rising to unexpected greatness at the right moment – Hurst for England in 1966, Mario Kempes for Argentina in 1978.

Hands up all those who think it was a goal. The scene at Wembley in 1966 as Geoff Hurst puts England back in front (or not) against West Germany in the World Cup Final

So Bobby Robson's squad should not be viewed too harshly in advance simply because it does not contain a Platini, a Maradona or a Karl-Heinz Rummenigge. Remember John Barnes's superb goal against Brazil in Rio in 1984. Here was an example of a promising young player suddenly responding to the magnificence of the setting and the challenge of the occasion. Forget the weakness of that particular Brazilian defence; Barnes still had to find the courage and skill to take them on.

The Watford player has not made the strides at international level heralded by this goal but there are others – Gary Lineker, Kerry Dixon, Mark Hateley for example – who could be touched by greatness in Monterrey. More predictably the fitness of Bryan Robson and the form and mood of Glenn Hoddle are going to be fundamental to England's success, as is the organisation of the defence around Terry Butcher and the safety of Peter Shilton's handling in goal.

If England reach the semi-finals, given the problems of playing in temperatures of around 100°F in Monterrey and readjusting to the higher altitude of the other venues, they will have done exceptionally well. If they are eliminated earlier, then judgement will depend on the manner of their departure, the opposition and what sort of luck they have experienced with injuries and referees.

Do we expect too much of England? It tends to be forgotten that the team does not represent football played in England, that mix of Anglo-Saxon and Celtic talents which gives our League much of its appeal, a mix now leavened by foreign players – with more and more Danes returning in search of new geld, paid this time in the hope that they will stay.

Or have we become conditioned into expecting too little? Take away 1966 and England have hardly prospered in the World Cup. They have never yet made it beyond the quarter-finals on foreign soil, and between 1970 and 1982 failed to qualify.

Until 1966, international pessimism had become deeply engrained where England were concerned. After all, if an England side containing Ramsey, Wright, Dickinson, Finney, Mannion and Mortensen could lose to the United States in the 1950 World Cup, what hope was there for their successors?

You have got to rate England's chances for 1986 slightly higher than their outlooks for 1954, 1958 and 1962. Indeed they did not start the 1966 competition as favourites: Portugal, Brazil and Hungary were fancied more strongly, although it was conceded that home advantage would probably take the hosts to the last four.

Seldom has a World Cup produced such an even-looking field, a point in England's favour. It is impossible to point to any country and argue a conclusive case for their winning the tournament. Of course the Latin-Americans will have certain advantages and Mexico, naturally acclimatised to the unusual conditions, ought to hold more sway than usual as the host nation, but, with the competition going into straight knock-out in the second round, form on any day is going to be even more important.

Just before the 1962 World Cup in Chile, Bobby Robson, who provided the pace in England's midfield, broke a bone in a foot and missed the whole tournament. If he is owed some luck at this level then surely his captain will not suffer a similar fate. Yet Bryan Robson pulled an already weakened hamstring in the decisive qualifying game against Turkey and lost momentum in Spain, after his marvellous start, because of a groin strain.

Three and a half years of varied team selections, changing patterns of play and mixed results have not altered the fact that Bryan Robson is the indispensable catalyst to the England side. When he is not playing it is as if the spark plugs have become oiled up; the team splutters and wheezes and makes fitful progress while emitting clouds of black exhaust.

The chemistry of the midfield has remained Bobby Robson's most persistent problem. In Denmark in 1982, facing the European Championship match which was his first after succeeding Ron Greenwood as manager, Robson stood up in Copenhagen and announced proudly that 'I've picked my team and we're coming to get you.'

True, England nearly won that match 2–1, but the image that stayed with Robson was of Olsen leaving his midfield and central defence for dead as he weaved through to score Denmark's late equaliser. The impression was confirmed at Wembley a year later when the Danes, though not at their best, were still good enough to win 1–0 and virtually end England's chances of qualifying for the European Championship finals in France. Needless to

Steve Coppell during his all-too-brief England career

Glenn Hoddle: few more gifted players in Mexico if the Tottenham man gets it right

say, Bryan Robson was missing from that game through injury.

Bobby Robson came away from Copenhagen thinking aloud about the need to get more tenacity and tackling power into England's midfield while at the same time creating movements of sufficient skill and subtlety to unsettle world-class defence.

With the former aim in mind he tried, among others, Mabbutt, Lee and Gregory but until Peter Reid of Everton came into the team during the 1985 summer tour in Mexico City there was little alternative to the authoritative, though at times passive, play of Ray Wilkins.

Another truth of Bobby Robson's tenure is that he has not found adequate successors to Trevor Brooking, Steve Coppell or the pre-1980 Kevin Keegan. The absence, at various times, of these three players proved too great a handicap for England in Spain when they saw a route to the semi-finals, and perhaps even the final, opening up before them, but failed to achieve the victory over the dejected hosts in Madrid that would have taken them along it.

Coppell missed that game with the knee injury that was to restrict his international career to two further appearances before he was forced into early retirement. Brooking and Keegan came on for the last 20 minutes – their only participation in the 1982 World Cup finals – and the latter missed a simple header.

The understanding between Brooking and Keegan, described by

Greenwood as 'telepathic', provided some of the best moments of England's football when they qualified for the 1980 European Championship in Italy. But, by the finals, Keegan was losing his pace and he never really regained it. His strength lay in coming quickly off defenders, demanding the ball short and instigating attacks with deft first-time touches. For a time he was England's most reliable finisher.

When Robson took over he saw the need for a clean break which would leave Bryan Robson more room to drive forward into scoring positions. Keegan took his omission badly and complained on the back page of the newspaper to which he was contracted. The England manager summed up the situation in one word: 'Tough!'

However, the continuing uncertainty about Bryan Robson's fitness and the failure of any player to fill the gap left by Brooking has made life equally tough for Bobby Robson. Glenn Hoddle is the best creative player available but until the 1985 tour tended to be regarded as an international icon – something to be carried amid much reverence but of little practical use.

Then Hoddle came on as substitute against Italy in the Aztec Stadium and so ordered things that his England career suddenly had fresh meaning. However acclimatised a team become in Mexico they cannot play their football in the helter-skelter English way.

The need to slow the game down, the fact that the midfields in Mexico are not likely to be cluttered by flying bodies and the importance of making possession count has put Hoddle in a completely different light. Not surprisingly he stayed in the England side for the rest of the qualifying competition.

No player was likely to fill Coppell's unique role as outside-cum-inside-right with a touch of the right-half thrown in. Trevor Steven of Everton is the nearest to him in style and effect but he has had to make way for the rise of Hoddle. Robson has flirted with the idea of two wingers but, given the inconsistency of Barnes and Waddle, has yet to find one. Moreover, England still miss Coppell's capacity for arriving in the goalmouth at precisely the right moment to collect rebounds and tap-ins. In ice hockey they are called 'garbage goals' – but they all count.

If World Cups are about anything they are about taking chances – or missing them (witness Astle in Guadalajara and Keegan in Madrid). Thus the argument comes back to the Linekers, the Hateleys and the Dixons. There is also Trevor Francis, but he no longer scores regularly, and Tony Woodcock, forever spinning, but whose England career is becoming lost in the windmills of the mind.

England's immediate problem may be more concerned with stopping goals being scored against them. Portugal, their first opponents in Monterrey, have Europe's leading scorer, Fernando Gomes, to lead their attack, and the Polish lancer, Boniek, has had more than a little success at club level in using his pace and finishing power to stun square English defences.

Spain '82: Jose Camacho (Spain) and Kenny Sansom (England) collide

True, England conceded only two goals in the qualifying competition but, in terms of the tournament proper, this statistic is as meaningless as the fact that they scored 21 (13 against the tremulous Turks). The well-being of Butcher and the effectiveness of his centre-back partnership with Terry Fenwick is crucial. At full-back Gary Stevens had a happier Mexican experience in 1985 than the more proven Kenny Sansom.

Shilton exudes massive reassurance but remember the long cross from Bagni of Italy in the Aztec Stadium that held its course in the thin atmosphere and sailed into the net above the England goalkeeper's head. At least the ball should behave itself in Monterrey.

You have to rate England's chances as fair to middling. It will be an arduous, exhausting tournament and one that should see the English players – accustomed to playing two highly competitive matches a week for nine months – holding some sort of advantage in terms of stamina. But it is how well they hold the ball that will determine their success or failure. Top-class football is quick to punish bad passing, and in the Mexican heat nobody with any sense is going to run if he can make the ball do the work.

PLATINI AND GIRESSE GET MICHEL SINGING LES BLEUS

DOMINIC ROUSSEAU

If 1984 will remain a historic year for French football – with the European Championship, gold medals in the Olympics, and a series of 12 victories in 12 games – 1985 has been less brilliant, even if France has managed to qualify for the World Cup finals for an unprecedented third time in a row. Dominique Rousseau of France's national sporting daily L'Equipe *discusses the latest developments.*

The diminution in confidence in the national team is due to two specific defeats – the first on 2 May in Sofia against Bulgaria (2–0) and the second on 11 September in Leipzig against East Germany (2–0 again). These two matches confirmed France's traditional inability to perform well away from home.

Later on in the year, during the last decisive qualifier on 16 November against Yugoslavia in the Parc des Princes, Les Bleus presented an aghast crowd with the spectacle of 68 minutes of almost total paralysis after Michel Platini had given them a third-minute lead. It was Platini, as usual their rescuer, who finally clinched victory with a second goal 19 minutes from the end.

In all those three matches, it was apparent that the team could still not work out whether to play an attacking game or a defensive one. It is a conundrum that has still not been resolved and which underpins the problems facing Henri Michel, the manager who took over from Michel

Michel Platini (France) takes avoiding action as John McClelland (N.Ireland) challenges

Henri Michel, France's man in charge of Platini & Co.

Hidalgo after the Europeans. Significantly, at half-time in Leipzig, when the score stood at 0–0, Michel asked his players to attack more, thus clashing with Platini and Alain Giresse who are still the side's most influential players.

Hidalgo avoided the problem simply by being prepared to consult the two men about tactical matters. But Michel, who before he took over had never before coached a side, is only 38, and as a former Nantes player and French international, an erstwhile team-mate of those he now has to mould into a national side. Clearly it is proving a problem for him since he has had some difficulty finding the right touch with players who, because of their age and experience, have most clout in the team.

But if France are having difficulties away from home then they are not the only ones, and Mexico will be neutral ground for all but the host country. Moreover, the knock-out system which will come into play from the quarter-finals onwards will be to their liking. After all, since losing the semi-final in Seville against West Germany in 1982, they have learned the crucial knack of winning despite playing badly. For a start, although it can hardly be overlooked that the European Championship took place on home soil, Les Bleus had to sweat for their victory. Only the match against

Spain '82: in the thick of the action with West Germany and France in their controversial semi-final. Six, Rocheteau and Karls fight for a victory that eventually went to West Germany on penalties

Spain '82: Kurt Welzl of Austria shoots past French sweeper Patrick Battiston

Belgium was anything like a triumph. Against Denmark, Yugoslavia, Portugal and Spain they proved that they did not need inspiration to win – and with them, paradoxically, it has been reliance on that quality which has proved their downfall in the past.

As far as team selection is concerned, the French line-up has changed very little since 1984 but one difficulty has arisen quite unexpectedly. A defence which had given away only 4 goals in 12 matches has lost its brio as a result of the conflicting claims of Max Bossis and Patrick Battiston to the role of libero.

Bossis, who played in that position in 1984, is now turning out for Racing Club de Paris in the Second Division and his inclusion can no longer be regarded as automatic. This is especially apparent since Battiston has been making such a mark at Bordeaux, the League champions of '84 and '85 and semi-finalists in the European Cup last year. Henri Michel has still not made up his mind, even playing them alongside one another against Yugoslavia, which clearly was not the ideal solution.

All the same, there has been one satisfaction – the continuing form of Joel Bats (Paris St Germain), who is considered to be one of the best keepers in Europe and who has amassed a record number of successive caps.

At right-back, William Ayache (Nantes) has secured his place thanks to his speed and the quality of his attacking play which fits in well with the French style.

In midfield, too, confidence remains. Fernandez, Tigana, Giresse and Platini make up a midfield which is the envy of almost every team in the world, even more so now that Fernandez has developed into such a complete player. Named as France's 1985 Player of the Year, he should prove one of the revelations of the World Cup. An energetic midfield grafter from Paris St Germain, his technical excellence and ability to co-ordinate the maelstrom of talents around him suggests a Gallic Billy Bremner.

Up front, traditionally the weakest part of the team, the partnership between Rocheteau (Paris St Germain) and Touré (Nantes) is the likely pairing in Mexico. Rocheteau has had a new lease of life this season at Paris St Germain, who are dominating this season's title race. For his part, Touré – nicknamed Le Brésilien – has fulfilled the promise of his technical talent and sheer physical prowess with Nantes in Europe this year.

Having used the recent weeks to make final adjustments to the team, Michel's squad arrive in Mexico after a fortnight's stay at Fort Romeu, their high-altitude training ground. By the start of the tournament, they will also have spent time at altitude in Santa Cruz de Tlaxcla and will be waiting for the kick-off in León.

Joel Bats, France's veteran goalkeeper

Aggressive play from Luis Fernandez (France)

ROSSI II

JOHN ROBERTS

What price the champions as Italy go for their second World Cup in a row? John Roberts of the Daily Mail *reports.*

According to John Charles, the noble Welsh giant who was all but canonized by Juventus a quarter of a century ago, Italy is really the only place to play football. The extremes of passion displayed there are addictive, he says, even though the subject of popular emotion is apt to be cast as a peasant one day, a king the next. Four years ago, Paolo Rossi played both roles with the aplomb of a Lord Olivier.

Spain '82: the end of the journey. Italy's hero Paolo Rossi brandishes the big prize

Enzo Bearzot, manager of Italy, with Paolo Rossi

As the Italians ascend to 7,400 feet to begin their defence of the World Cup in the Aztec Stadium, Mexico's showpiece for the 1986 tournament, the image of Rossi in his moment of fulfilment remains strong. So, too, does the memory of a slender, haunted young man, overburdened with responsibility and wearing a look of desperate isolation even when surrounded by comrades. This was the Rossi of Pontevedra, where the Italians made camp in the extreme northwest corner of Spain in the summer of 1982.

He was 25 years old then, this waif of Italian sport, and had cause to adopt the demeanour of a condemned man. He had only recently been released after serving a two-year suspension ordered by the same Italian Football Federation that now expected him to perform wonders on the field for his country as an act of atonement. He had been found guilty of taking a bribe from a greengrocer who was a member of an illegal betting ring involved in fixing matches. Two years of an incredible goal-scoring career that first caught the world's attention in Argentina in 1978 had been squandered (even at the time of the ban his transfer value was estimated to be £3 million).

In a sense, Rossi was destined to be one of football's mavericks almost from the moment he became a professional player. Juventus despaired of his frailty after three operations on his knees and farmed him out to Como, Lanerossi Vicenza, with whom his play burgeoned and his fame grew, and Perugia, for whom he was playing when the scandal broke. When his sentence was served, Juventus reclaimed him.

As the Italians trained in Pontevedra, Rossi, number 20, gave the impression of a prisoner on parole hoping to remove a stain from his character. His preparation for the tournament had been sparse to say the least: two matches for Juventus, in which he at least managed to score a goal, and one game for the national team, a 'friendly' encounter in Switzerland.

There was discernible testiness between Enzo Bearzot, the Italian team manager, and some members of the media whose role, they seem to imagine, transcends the typewriter and microphone and impinges on the manager's preserve of team selection. There was a fair amount of swaggering in waterproof, lightweight jackets provided for the Press by the Italian leisurewear company, Ellesse, and much mumbling of impending doom. Bearzot, gaunt and careworn, attempted to ignore the impertinence. He knew better than anyone that this was nothing compared to the scorn of a nation that would accompany failure.

Rossi aside, most interest was attracted by Italy's goalkeeper and captain, Dino Zoff, who, at the age of 40, was about to start the tournament by making his 100th appearance for his country. Two understudies, Ivano Bordon and Giovanni Galli, were resigned to seats as spectators. Zoff had not missed a single League match since joining Juventus ten years earlier. 'His secret is humility,' Bearzot said, adding, as if with the reporters in mind, 'He doesn't think he knows it all.'

The doubters remained in the ascendancy throughout the opening phase of the tournament. The Italians would leave their hotel and travel a few miles south to Vigo in hope, only to return in a state of depression. A goalless draw with Poland set the pattern. The Italians ought to have won, and but for an interception by Gregorz Lato and a header that passed agonisingly wide of a post Rossi would have ensured that they did. As it was, neurosis began to set in.

Rossi, who had done enough against the Poles to suggest that he needed only the impetus of a goal to restore his confidence, was so chronically inept against Peru that Bearzot was forced to retire him at half-time. His place was taken by the ageing Franco Causio, and the paucity of Italy's attacking potential was such that the partnership of the angular Francesco Graziani and Causio was reminiscent of Don Quixote and Sancho Panza. A 1-1 draw did not represent much of a tilt.

Fortunately for Italy their rivals were suffering from a similar malaise. Indeed, Group One seemed in need of group therapy until Poland found form and beat Peru 5–1 in La Coruna. Italy, needing a goalless draw against Cameroon to qualify for the second phase as runners-up to the Poles, stumbled on. The score was 1–1, chiefly because the African goalkeeper, Thomas N'Kono, lost his balance at a vital moment. Frankly, Cameroon failed to respond to an opportunity to cause the biggest sensation since North Korea in 1966.

So what went right? The Italian transformation in Barcelona and subsequent triumph in Madrid could be attributed to many factors. For one thing, they had backed themselves into a corner from which the only means of escape was to overcome the dread of losing by allowing their abundant talent to flow. For another thing, the quality of opposition may have helped concentrate their minds. Several players had distinguished themselves from the outset, Gaetano Scirea, the libero, and Bruno Conti, the right-

Spain '82: Michael Kaham (Cameroons) and Paolo Rossi (Italy) help fight out a questionable 1–1 draw

Ossie in Barcelona ... Ardiles of Tottenham and Argentina keeps his eye on Italy's Bruno Conti

Spain '82: Alberto Tarantini (Argentina) feels the quality of Sandro Altobelli's shirt during Italy's 2–1 victory

winger, in particular. In Barcelona, the others responded. Giancarlo Antognoni and Marco Tardelli were artist and dealer respectively in midfield and Rossi, restored immediately following his débâcle against Peru, finally rediscovered the way to goal.

Argentina, the holders, were beaten, 2–1, in a match which, as was remarked at the time, contained all the exaggerated violence of a spaghetti western and the acting was better. In contrast, the match with Brazil was a celebration of the football riches Europe and Latin America could produce. Italy won, 3–2, with Rossi's first goals, a hat-trick; he was lost and was found again.

Before the semi-final against Poland the Italian players called a strike against the Press, withdrawing their co-operation because of reports that they had each received £35,000 for reaching the second round when the actual figure was £8,000. Dario Bianchi, the squad's long-suffering administrator, gave a shrug and said, 'The Italian Press and public are always the same. If we lose against Poland we will be no bloody good again.'

With the potential menace of Zbigniew Boniek removed by suspension, there seemed little likelihood of Italy being beaten by the Poles. And by this time Rossi was irresistible. His two goals took Italy to Madrid for the final against West Germany, who had won few friends by showing too much charity towards the Austrians and not enough toward the French. Italy won, 3–1, to equal Brazil's record of three World Cup triumphs. Rossi scored one of the goals to finish as the tournament's top scorer with six and was voted Man of the Match.

One up and two to go: Paolo Rossi celebrates Italy's opening goal against West Germany in the Spain '82 final

Since then Italian football has evolved into the choicest cosmopolitan mixture on earth, a League laced with international excellence. Not long ago, however, a rather special domestic transfer caught the public's interest. The national hero was released by Juventus and moved on to AC Milan, whose supporters insisted that the romantic story would have a sequel and that the world should prepare for Rossi II.

BIG PAT AND COMPANY AREN'T NO-HOPERS NOW

ROBERT ARMSTRONG

Foreign journalists are always bemused by Northern Ireland. Not so Robert Armstrong of the Guardian *who was at their side during their last fabulous Cup run in Spain.*

Four years ago when the Irish were preparing near Valencia for the World Cup finals the Spanish press would ask Billy Bingham 'Why do you allow your players to spend the afternoon sunbathing? Why do they drink beer after training? Why does the goalkeeper [Jim Platt] have his wife with him?'

The Spanish might also have asked why the Irish team gave the British press so much pleasure by taking on overweight reporters at tennis and five-a-side football in the car park of the Hotel Sidi Saler Sol. The answer is simple: neither Bingham nor his players spend a moment worrying about the quality of the opposition, whether it be Spain, West Germany, or a local amateur team engaged for a 40-minute practice.

In fact the Northern Ireland style is the realisation of a journalist's dream. Anyone who has travelled with other international squads quickly becomes aware of the tight-lipped, almost sullen atmosphere that surrounds an important match. A trip with the Irish makes a delightful contrast, full of humour, off-the-cuff chat and friendly banter among the players. Everyone enjoys himself.

Victory over Romania. Billy Bingham expresses his feelings to Pat Jennings

In his 113th match (a world record) for N. Ireland, Pat Jennings frustrates an England attack

Consider the case of Pat Jennings who was declared 'over the hill' by several reporters way back in 1977 when the Irish lost 5–0 in Cologne to West Germany. Last October Big Pat gave a world-class performance in Bucharest where Northern Ireland's 1–0 win over Romania took them to within a point of the 1986 World Cup finals.

Afterwards Jennings chatted about the charity golf tournament he was about to set off to play in Spain with Severiano Ballesteros. 'Never mind the hype, let's get on with the fun' was his message.

If the keynote of the Irish approach is relaxation off the pitch, the degree of application during training is a rigorous contrast. Bingham rehearses set pieces many times over, gives individuals specific tasks during practice matches, and insists on a level of physical fitness that has led to more than one senior player losing his place in the past. Wee Billy gives short shrift to slackers.

Bingham requires intense commitment but that is not to imply that the Irish squad lacks quality. One of the enduring myths Northern Ireland has to bear is the media caricature of a team of no-hopers from the lower divisions who combine passion and good fortune in equal measure to inflict upsets on the aristocrats of football.

Such an image is actually a patronising insult to one half of the squad and a misleading assessment of the ability of the other half. Of course, the Irish can play with heart and pride but so can England when pitted against say West Germany or Scotland or Brazil. It is often forgotten that Northern Ireland, just like England, can drift into a listless muddle against the minnows of international football. Witness that despairing defeat in Finland in 1984 and their passionless and goalless draw in Turkey only last September. The Irish know the dog days as intimately as the moments of glory.

The paradox of Northern Ireland in recent years is that the squad has included players worth a place in most national teams – Jennings, Norman Whiteside, Martin O'Neill, Mal Donaghy, John McClelland – yet they always prefer to be regarded as the underdogs. Whenever the Irish are expected to win they invariably struggle as they did before defeating Finland 2–1 in a jittery return game in Belfast in 1984.

Outside observers often find Northern Ireland's powerful cadre spirit difficult to explain because of the religious divisions that have torn the province apart. The fact is that Ulstermen generally have more in common with each other than with the citizens of either England or the Republic of Ireland. The British National Anthem may cause some Catholics private twinges but professional footballers tend to make common cause against a common enemy.

In any case the single most compelling reason for Northern Ireland's place in the 1986 World Cup finals is to be found in the personality of their 53-year-old manager. Since Bingham took charge of the squad for the second time in January 1980, the Irish have lost only 13 out of a total of 48 games, usually by a single goal and very rarely by more than two. For a manager who draws his players from a population of one million people that is an astonishing record of success.

In his more candid moments Bingham will sometimes hint that he does not have players of sufficient quality to give maximum effect to his tactics. Yet the Irish have claimed some of the most prestigious scalps in European football, including those of Spain, West Germany (twice), Austria, Scotland, Romania (twice) and Portugal. It is worth noting that four of those nations have reached the Mexico finals, with Spain drawn once again in Northern Ireland's group along with Algeria and Brazil.

'I think the sum total of my experiences over many years enables me to make better decisions now,' says Bingham. 'I used to make more mistakes in my first period as manager for Northern Ireland in the late sixties but today I am sensitive about when to face things at team talks and when not to – I never labour deficiencies, I boost morale, and I know enough about the game to be credible to players.'

Bingham will happily admit the opposition to his training sessions where he is renowned for his meticulous attention to detail. In Bucharest the Romanian coach visited the Irish camp, took copious notes, made diagrams, and later complained bitterly that the presence of Harry Cavan, a FIFA vice-president, had intimidated the referee into allowing the Irish to win before 70,000 fans in the 23 August stadium.

Any Irish squad is bound to carry its fair share of tearaways – Bobby

The man with a hard act to follow: N.Ireland's reserve goalie Jim Platt

Spain '82: Austrian goalie Friedrich Koncilia refuses to believe it as Billy Hamilton celebrates

Campbell and Terry Cochrane spring to mind – but discipline has never presented a major problem for Bingham. During the 1982 finals Jim Platt threatened to pull out of the squad if he was not picked, but he stayed on and eventually played two games when Jennings dropped out with a groin injury. Billy Hamilton and Sammy Nelson kept their places despite a private punch-up which left Nelson looking like an advert for Elastoplast.

Bingham prefers self-discipline because it is the vital element in Northern Ireland's tactical style. Having tasted World Cup success as a right-winger in the 1958 finals, Wee Billy has always been keenly aware that international football requires a high level of physical and mental concentration. The low-scoring profile of the Irish team since 1980 – 42 goals for, 41 against – reflects the tight, organised character of the man from East Belfast.

However, Mexico is certain to present a unique challenge to the Northern Ireland squad that could tax some players beyond their physical capacity. The intense heat and the high altitude of Guadalajara are likely to prove a gruelling experience for a squad that has never played a competitive game outside Europe. The Irish will attempt to acclimatise by spending two and a half weeks in New Mexico training on the campus of the University of Albuquerque.

Bingham has cause to feel optimistic about the match against Spain, who have failed to beat the Irish in their last three meetings, most recently in a 0–0 friendly in Majorca in March 1985. But neither Algeria nor Brazil has ever encountered Northern Ireland whose acquaintance with Central and South American nations has been restricted to friendlies in Belfast against Mexico and Uruguay and a World Cup game against Argentina in Sweden in 1958.

Indeed, it is a familiar scenario for the Irish – an unfriendly climate, powerful opposition, and long odds on reaching the second round. In theory, Bingham's men should finish no higher than third in their group, though that could be good enough for further progress as one of the four best third-placed nations in terms of points and goals. Of course, Algeria, who scored a sensational win over West Germany in the 1982 finals, will not be content merely to finish as also-rans. The African nation, coached significantly by a Brazilian, will be a dangerous floater amongst the élite.

Even so, the Irish can call upon an exceptional range of experience in all positions, though Bingham has taken care to introduce half a dozen men to the squad in their early twenties within the past two years. It will be interesting to see whether Jennings actually plays in Mexico a month before his 41st birthday with the two Irish League goalkeepers, Platt (Coleraine) and George Dunlop (Linfield) both eager to take his place.

Northern Ireland's defence is one of the most consistent in Europe, having conceded just one goal in six matches played in 1985. There is sharp competition for the two centre-back positions from John O'Neill, McClelland and Alan McDonald, the QPR man who made a splendid debut in Bucharest and carried on his solid work against England. Jimmy

Norman Whiteside of Manchester United and N.Ireland caught in typically determined mood

Max Bossis polices Gerry Armstrong as France defeat N.Ireland 4–1 in Spain '82

Nicholl, Donaghy and Nigel Worthington have all performed with conviction at full-back in the past 18 months.

While the Irish squad, especially in midfield, could be criticised for including half a dozen players aged 30 or over, there is no doubt that the youngest man, Norman Whiteside, still only 20, exerts a strategic influence wholly out of proportion to his years. Since Whiteside has withdrawn from attack to midfield – for both Manchester United and Northern Ireland – the prolonged absence of Martin O'Neill with a knee injury has scarcely been noticed. The return of David McCreery at the expense of Gerry Armstrong (who has been an excellent substitute) has brought extra steel to the middle.

Scoring remains Northern Ireland's greatest problem, with a dismal average of rather less than a goal a game over the past six years. The withdrawal of Armstrong (11 goals) and the positional switch of Whiteside (7 goals) has deprived the attack of Northern Ireland's two leading marksmen. It is to be hoped that Hamilton will recover from his persistent knee injury in time to link up with Jimmy Quinn, the Blackburn striker who scored the winner in Romania. Meanwhile, the presence of two specialist wingers, Ian Stewart and Stephen Penney, gives the attack an air of promise if not fulfilment.

As Northern Ireland approach their third World Cup finals in 28 years it is worth pointing out that their mere presence in Mexico is sufficient to send a powerful charge of excitement through all Irishmen. In 1982 messages of goodwill were sent to Bingham from the Government of the Republic of Ireland and in 1986 Dublin's good wishes will carry extra significance in the light of the Anglo-Irish Agreement. Football is proving that it can still be the agent of reconciliation, at least on one side of the Irish Sea.

THE SKY'S THE LIMIT FOR THE MEN IN RED AND WHITE

KAZ MOCHLINSKI

Poland enter the 13th World Cup finals as one of the six seeded teams, albeit seemingly the weakest and least favoured of the six. Kaz Mochlinski looks at their chances.

It is a completely just reward for the Poles' fine performances in the World Cup competitions of recent years, and particularly for reaching the semi-finals of the last Mundial in Spain in 1982. Having qualified for the finals only once before the 1974 event in West Germany, they have since finished in third place twice. And though detractors may point to those results having been achieved in Europe, it took Brazil and hosts Argentina to eliminate them from the 1978 competition in the second round. Now Poland embark on their fourth consecutive final appearance with a fear that their best players are too old and that a new crop of brilliant youngsters are not yet mature or experienced enough.

There has been an ever-growing interest in the great Mexican fiesta to come; this reached a peak after the draw in December, since when hardly a day has passed without leading articles in the newspapers about the World Cup and the national team. For a long time before the announcement of the seeds and where they were to play, the Poles were pessimistically certain that they would draw the short straw and have to play as seeds in Monterrey.

While Franz Beckenbauer was reserving accommodation near Querétaro, the Poles originally thought that the Organising Committee of 'Mexico '86' had put them in León and France in Monterrey – a logical step since Monterrey is around three times as large as León. While France could expect a few thousand supporters to follow them, there was little chance of more than a hundred Polish fans coming to Mexico with their team. But when the French visited Monterrey and experienced the climate, they set in motion their bureaucratic machinery to change their venue; and with none of the big nations willing to move, Poland – without any representation in the hierarchy of either FIFA or UEFA – was relocated.

They have at least played well there before, beating Mexico 2–1 at the Tecnológico Stadium in 1973 under Kazimierz Gorski. He stressed the

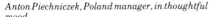

Anton Piechniczek, Poland manager, in thoughtful mood

Poland's keeper, Jozef Mlynarczyk

importance of medical help in preparing players physically, including doctors in his regular conferences with trainers. Now Anton Piechniczek, the Pole's 38-year-old manager and former international, has followed his predecessor's approach, putting great emphasis on the physical condition of his players, with their fitness being almost as great a determining factor in their selection as their ability. After visiting Monterrey in December with his colleagues, Piechniczek declared that the results in the World Cup would depend to a great extent on the physical condition of the players and that he intended to choose players who could give their all in the frequent matches in intense heat and humidity. To this end, three doctors – specialists in physical regeneration – were present at squad training, daily monitoring each player's physiology.

One consolation at least is Monterrey's proximity to the US, from where many exiled Poles are expected to travel to watch the 'Men in Red and White', and even perhaps to outnumber English supporters. But not many are thought to be able to afford the prices to travel from Poland, though the cost is around less than a third of that being charged in Britain.

They will see a team much changed from that envisaged at the start of the campaign. Piechniczek is far more open about the national team than Bobby Robson, who has been made wary in the extreme by a critical public and media dogmatic in their desire for objectivity. Before the first qualifying matches Piechniczek outlined his problems, particularly the lack of both full-backs, two midfielders, and an attacker. As the group matches have progressed, these problem positions have changed, as young players have emerged to fill these gaps, but others have aged and new weaknesses became apparent.

Poland play basically a 4–4–2 system, with two normal stopper-centre halves, and a midfield with one defensive helper and one man supporting the forwards flanked by two wide players. Gornik Zabrze and Legia Warszawa, the country's most successful club sides of the last 30 years, supply the bulk of the national squad, including a number of the star performers, though the two best players, Jozef Mlynarczyk and Zbigniew Boniek, play for overseas clubs. This is regarded as something of a disadvantage as they are unable to participate in all the squad sessions and practice matches.

Placing a reliance on men who gained experience in Spain four years ago, Piechniczek's surest position is the goalkeeper's, where despite his age (32½) Jozef Mlynarczyk is still unchallenged. When he moved from Widzew Lodz to the Corsican club Bastia he proved he was one of the best goalkeepers in Europe and became very popular with the French. He regretted having to leave Bastia at the end of last year after they got into terrible financial difficulties and he was not paid for three months. But on moving to F.C. Porto in Portugal he was greeted with adulation; some 2,500 people turned up to see his first training session, and a record crowd of almost 120,000 came to watch his debut against Benfica in Lisbon.

But though a fine performance and clean sheet brought more acclaim, there are those who question whether he can last the pace in Mexico, and there are no ready reserves. Jan Kazimierski let in five goals last year in Mexico, and Eugeniusz Cebrat was ousted this season from his club place by the promising Jozef Wandzik who, though 22 now, is likely to be Mlynarczyk's successor. Even Chelsea's highly regarded Eddi Niedzwiecki was considered until being capped by Wales.

Poland is fortunate in having two fine full-backs, though both are very different in character. On the right side, Krzysztof Pawlak of Lech Poznan may be unspectacular but he is solid and dependable. On the other hand, Pogon Szczecin's left-back Marek Ostrowski is quick and intelligent, with a splendid long shot. He showed this in scoring the vital goal in Athens to put Poland 2–1 up against Greece, which gave them the impetus to win 4–1 and gain the goal difference to go through to Mexico, in their best match in four years under Piechniczek.

The central defence will be without Wladyslaw Zmuda, formerly of Widzew and Verona and now with Cremonese in Italy. Just short of his century of caps, age and consequent loss of pace and turning ability counted against him, and a fierce battle is in progress to partner the tall Widzew defender Roman Wojcicki. Particularly accomplished in the air and a good marker, Wojcicki played throughout all but one of Poland's full internationals last year. His club colleague, Kazimierz Przybys, has pace,

Spain '82: Zbigniew Boniek in the hunt as Cameroon's Elie Onana attacks

but the slightly stronger Waldemar Waleszczyk of Ruch Chorzow is more experienced as a centre-half, though he came late into the reckoning.

They will be aided by Waldemar Matysik, one of the national side's top men and a Player of the Year in 1985. Ambitious and a brave battler, the defensive midfielder is one of the backbones of 1985 champions Gornik Zabrze, and played in all of Poland's qualifying games. Those playing in front of him are subject to change during the matches in Mexico, as many combinations are possible, with men like Zbigniew Boniek and Dariusz Dziekanowski being able to play both in the centre of the pitch and up front. Probably Jan Urban from Gornik, who in the past year forced his way up from the junior side and possesses a great shot, will play in left midfield. On the right Andrzej Buncol (Legia) is experienced, and has excellent ball control, boasting the ability to keep the ball in motion a few centimetres from his feet.

But Boniek is the key to the team. One of the greatest footballers Poland has produced, his mane of red hair (prompting the nickname 'Red Devil') is instantly recognisable to every Pole. Now playing for A.S. Roma after leaving Juventus last summer, he is inspirational to those around him as well as being capable of individual brilliance.

Boniek is renowned for his touch and speed, and also has a fearsome shot. But while he will be playing in his third finals, the country's new star Dziekanowski will be making his debut. An excellent dribbler and shooter, he is one of the most talented and creative footballers in Poland. He is also a great solo player, as he showed in Athens with a brilliant move for the fourth goal which ensured qualification for the finals. He greatly impressed officials of Inter Milan this season, when he played against them in the UEFA Cup. The player and trainer will have to decide whether he plays up front with Boniek, and if he does, his Legia Warszawa club colleague Jan Karas could come in as a support player, though he lost his place in the club side this season.

Dziekanowski's position up front could come as result of Wlodzimierz Smolarek's poor form this season, though Piechniczek has great faith in his internationally proven players and the Widzew raider was one of the heroes of the last finals. The amiable Smolarek only played with Dziekanowski in the qualifying rounds as on the field they temporarily put aside their personal conflict which caused the latter to leave Widzew for Legia last year. Andrzej Palasz is another option, but though a willing and frequent shooter, he scores proportionally few goals.

The League's most consistent scorer, Andrzej Zgutczynski – another Gornik star like Palasz – lacks international experience and is therefore considered a risk in the top matches. So is the up-and-coming 20-year-old Andrzej Rudy of Slask Wroclaw who, though uncapped, is highly rated by Piechniczek and an able play-maker. His club partner in the middle of the park, Ryszard Tarasiewicz, has been given a run-out in the international side, but many feel he has not yet been allowed enough opportunity to demonstrate his developing skills and is more likely to be employed as substitute.

Surprisingly uncertain even about his squad place is the Lech forward Miroslaw Okonski, who tempted Gunther Netzer to Poznan to sign him to play for Hamburg S.V. in the Bundesliga next season. There's also uncertainty about Gornik's Ryszard Komornicki, the intelligent and technically skilled midfielder who is, however, hampered by poor physique, which may rule him out with Piechniczek seeking peak physical condition in the players who will participate in the World Cup.

Despite this abundance of quality players, the management is pessimistic about finding the right blend and, moreover, about being able to acclimatise and then perhaps make the transition to higher altitude – if they get that far. For while the fans believe the sky's the limit (and there is great expectancy in the country), those involved with the squad have a nagging feeling that England, whom they rate as one of the world's top teams, may avenge themselves for the events of 17 October 1973. But with Boniek particularly seeking to climax his illustrious career on a high note, there may well be smiles on Polish faces come the end of June.

THE SIDE THAT JOCK BUILT REVEALS THE TRUE FLOWER OF SCOTLAND

PATRICK BARCLAY

Once the butt of international football, now (thanks to the late Jock Stein) a highly respected side, Scotland face Mexico knowing they have the worst draw of all. But can they still go far? Patrick Barclay analyses their past and future.

Scotland's place in the finals came at too high a price, as the supporters trudging through the subdued streets of Cardiff on the night of 10 September made clear. It cost the life of Jock Stein, his heart defeated by the 1–1 draw that revived his team's chances of qualification.

A few days earlier, with Britain sensitive to the need for good crowd behaviour in the wake of Brussels, Stein had asked supporters to remember that the crunch meeting in Group Seven was 'just a football match'. But the Big Man could not protect himself; for Stein the strains were direct and unavoidable. He had already shown discomfort, to the concern of lieutenants on the bench, before Davie Cooper's late equaliser from a disputed penalty sent the tartan terraces wild. Twenty thousand Scots danced to the final whistle and beyond. Most had left when the news filtered through from a treatment room in Ninian Park's main stand: Jock Stein was dead.

A nation went numb. The solemn faces of supporters, interviewed on television, contrasted poignantly with the jaunty tammies they still wore. Wasn't it somehow appropriate, prompted the interviewer, that Stein's last match had kept Scotland on the road to Mexico? 'Ah wish we werenae gaun,' came the reply, 'and Jock was staying hame wi' us.' It is nevertheless worth noting that Stein's last ploy had been to introduce Cooper, whose wing skills invigorated Scotland in the spell leading to his equaliser.

Thus goal difference, the quadrennial bane of Scottish World Cup hopes, did them a favour for once in edging out the unlucky Welsh, who three months later must have choked over the meal Scotland made of the ensuing play-off against Australia. Scotland gave only one truly convincing performance along their tortuous and tragic route to Mexico. They were superb against Spain at Hampden Park, winning 3–1 with the aid of an impeccably timed shaft of virtuosity from Kenny Dalglish. The rest of their football was all too often scrambled, tentative, and woefully lacking in the teamwork that seemed to come naturally to Wales. They were, in short, very fortunate to qualify.

The journey to Mexico via Seville, Reykjavik, Cardiff and Melbourne began in Glasgow on 17 October 1984 amid an atmosphere of confidence generated by a 6–1 victory over Yugoslavia on the same Hampden pitch a month earlier. That, however, was a friendly and Iceland, on World Cup duty, proved more earnest. But Paul McStay, just 20, led Scotland away from danger with his first two international goals, the latter a stunning drive from long range, and Charlie Nicholas completed a satisfactory 3–0 win after replacing Dalglish.

The next month brought the visit of Spain, their stock high after finishing second to France in the European Championship, then opening their World Cup account with a 3–0 victory over Wales in which Butragueno made an ominous debut. But they couldn't handle Scotland who, as occasionally happens, played as a team. After Mo Johnston had twice headed home, Goicoechea's reply brought a splendid response from Dalglish, who worked his way infield from the right, waited patiently for a gap, and curled a lovely shot beyond Arconada. What a way for the old maestro to equal Denis Law's record of 30 goals for Scotland; and what was more, after giving way to Nicholas in the previous two matches, he lasted the full 90 minutes.

Even the English had to take notice of such a performance. On television Greavsie joined the Saint in drooling over the likes of Cooper and Jim Bett, hitherto far-off names of which he had known little. Was this the team all Britain had been waiting for since Seeler, Muller, Grabowski, and company had laid Ramsey's era to rest in Mexico 14 years earlier? Certainly the Scots would qualify. It was two out of four, and Wales could be discounted after losing in Iceland and Spain. Scotland, however, had other ideas. But first the gods had an idea. Scotland went to Seville on 27 February 1985 hoping to field an unchanged side. But an hour before kick-off at the towering Sanchez Pizjuan stadium, with a capacity crowd of 70,000 already building the most fervent, hostile atmosphere this correspondent has experienced, Stein announced that Dalglish and Steve Nicol would miss the match having failed to recover from a secret bout of flu or something similar. Nicol was ably replaced by Richard Gough, but Dalglish left an unbridgeable gap; his former Liverpool comrade Graeme Souness, Scotland's captain, looked half the man he had been at Hampden. With the exceptions of Gough, Cooper, and the goalkeeper, Jim Leighton, whose nerve survived a constant barrage of missiles, the Scots did little to gainsay their reputation as bad travellers in a 1–0 defeat by a moderate Spanish side. Steve Archibald, being the Spanish League's leading goalscorer at the time, may have seemed a reasonable replacement for Dalglish; in the event his flaccidity was emphasised by Fernando Clos, his unsung partner at Barcelona, who headed the winner in masterly style.

Never mind, said the Scots. It's only another month till Wales come to Glasgow and we can put matters right. Well, Wales came, saw, and

The late Jock Stein – a too-high price for Scotland

Spain '82: Steve Archibald of Scotland and Barcelona in action

conquered. While they prepared for the match Mike England, their manager, made no attempt to hide media comments about Rush, Hughes, Southall and Ratcliffe constituting a four-man team (though wiser Scottish counsels reflected that, if Scotland had those four men, they would be thinking not only of qualifying for the World Cup, but of winning it). The Welsh resolved to rebut those comments, which they did by strangling the Scots' midfield – Souness was driven so deep by Phillips he almost drowned – and mangling their defence. Rush scored a sensational winner, but the roughing-up Hughes gave Alex McLeish and Willie Miller will remain as long in the memory. For all that, Scotland surrendered too easily. They thought the football they had imposed on Spain would be enough and, when it wasn't, floundered. Not for the first time, the nation that likes to think it has fire in its belly was exposed as the White Feather Club.

After recovering some pride, and paying their dues to the Hampden faithful, with a narrow victory in the annual joust with England – Gough's headed goal emphasising what a handy lad he is to have around in a crisis – they flew immediately to Reykjavik to pick up the threads of the World Cup campaign. In the meantime Wales had increased the pressure by exceeding Scotland's best achievement with a 3–0 victory over Spain at Wrexham. This meant that Scotland had to beat Iceland, a far from negligible side under their English manager, Tony Knapp, or face having to win their final match in Cardiff. They found the May conditions in Iceland more amenable than Wales had endured eight months earlier. But Dalglish was missing again, preparing with Liverpool for the horror of the following night in

Kenny Dalglish, pride of Anfield and Scotland   *The bravery and power of Scotland's Andy Gray*

Brussels, and, with Johnston another absentee, Stein had to gamble up front on Andy Gray, pairing the old warhorse with his Everton clubmate Graeme Sharp, an international debutant. Again Scotland played unimpressively. They were hauled out of trouble by Leighton, who saved a penalty. 'The eternal verities are challenged,' muttered one eminent Scot in the press box. 'We've found a goalkeeper.' We thought they might escape with a goalless draw, relatively respectable if inadequate. Then Gordon Strachan crossed; Archibald, a substitute for Gray, appeared to flap a hand at the ball; but the referee saw nothing and Bett appeared at the far post to score. His first international goal seemed nothing short of miraculous.

It was now a question of drawing with Wales. Souness was out, suspended, having acquired his second caution of the series in Reykjavik, and as the great day approached it became clear that Dalglish would also be absent, injured. On the eve of the match the ailing Stein, his grey face showing the tension all committed Scots had felt for months, announced a team featuring two markers, McLeish and Gough, designed to combat Rush and Hughes with the help of a sweeper, Miller. The midfield positions went to Strachan, Bett, and the tough Roy Aitken, with Sharp and David Speedie each making second international appearances up front. Wales were the more experienced side and, on recent evidence, by far the more capable: an impression confirmed when they took the lead in the 14th minute, Peter Nicholas bursting past two hesitant defenders to cross for the lethal Hughes. But Scotland pulled themselves together, showing all the combative spirit they had lacked at Hampden. They played no football to speak of, but the sheer persistence exemplified by Aitken and Speedie, allied to the astute introduction of Cooper, saw them arm-wrestle towards ascendancy. They deserved a draw, and their Icelandic luck returned to deliver it when Speedie turned the ball against Philips's hand, earning a much debated penalty. The final nine minutes were frantic, and as the excitement mounted a group of photographers, eager to portray Stein in his moment of triumph, crowded in on the bench. Half an hour later, Stein was dead.

The SFA turned to his assistant, the highly successful Aberdeen manager Alex Ferguson, who agreed initially to take charge for an October friendly against East Germany. Despite the welcome presence of both Souness and Dalglish this was a goalless and inconclusive affair, far less encouraging than the pre-match news that Ferguson would extend his period of office until the conclusion of the World Cup campaign, whenever and wherever that might be; Scotland, by finishing second in their group, now faced a two-legged play-off against the winners of the Oceania group, Australia. The abrasive Antipodeans came to Hampden first and proved as frustrating as their manager, Frank 'Mad Dog' Arok, had promised. But Cooper broke through with a free-kick and minutes later, lo and behold, a Scottish striker scored a goal: the first feat of its kind since Dalglish beat Arconada. Dalglish headed through, and the debutant Frank McAvennie tickled the ball past Australia's goalkeeper to give Scotland a 2–0 lead. The Glasgow press felt this would be enough, but suspicions to the contrary were strengthened when Ferguson's depleted squad made the long journey to Melbourne. They lacked several English-based players, including Dalglish and Strachan, and Souness arrived from Genoa only 36 hours before the match. Such a build-up, fraught with club–country negotiations, did little for the dignity of the world's major competition. And Scotland once again let themselves down before a nationwide breakfast-time audience back home on Channel Four. Only a brilliant save by Leighton prevented Australia from going in at half-time with a merited lead, after which the Scots stumbled through to another goalless draw and a place in the finals.

Their defence had conceded only one goal, Hughes's in Cardiff, in six matches since the shocking defeat by Wales at Hampden. In the process they discovered that they had a goalkeeper. But little else stood on the credit side of the balance sheet. Their best players, Dalglish and Souness, were ageing and although they had tried any number of strikers – Dalglish, Johnston, McAvennie, Sharp, Speedie, Gray, Archibald, Nicholas – a penetrative combination had still to emerge. They left Melbourne looking less of a team, and more of a collection of players, than when embarking upon the odyssey against Iceland at Hampden 14 months earlier. The nation can, however, take pride in having survived the qualifying stages of a World Cup for the fourth time in succession – a feat equalled by few countries (Winterbottom's England among them) and exceeded only by West Germany and Mexico. They had not proved capable of topping their group, as in the previous campaign under Stein, but hope springs eternal that a beast of a draw – setting them against West Germany, Uruguay and Denmark – will remove inhibitions and reveal the true flower of Scotland.

ASIAN MINNOWS LOOKING FOR GOALS AND GLORY

GORDON BORELAND

Glory in sport, especially in soccer, often brings forth a precocious partisanship in fledgeling nations. Gordon Boreland looks at one side who need to improve on their first experience of life in the World Cup – South Korea.

Few forget the verbal cartwheels of the Norwegian commentator who serenaded Mrs Thatcher, Princess Diana and even Sir Winston Churchill when the referee blew the final whistle in Oslo after Norway had inflicted a 2–1 defeat on an England side that seemed at the time to be sliding inexorably out of World Cup contention.

South Korean newspapermen are clearly worthy successors to the Scandinavian encomiast. Not for them the dull platitudes of detachment, the insincere tributes to the other team that give English football journalism its insipid objectivity. No, when South Korea met Japan in the first leg of the deciding game in the East Asian qualifiers, their 2–1 victory was accorded its proper due as a 'thrashing'.

But if they can find a few moments of rest from their intensive physical preparation for the finals, the South Korean squad will review previous tournaments with rather more ambivalent feelings.

They have the distinction of being the first Asian nation to qualify for the finals in the modern soccer era. But their visit to Switzerland in 1954 was fleeting, for they conceded 16 goals without reply to the wizardly Hungarians and not so esteemed Turks.

A second statistic is more intriguing and will tantalise the South Koreans unless they still hold grudges over the bloody events of 1953. For it was their northern neighbours and former adversaries North Korea who in 1966 dished up one of the biggest surprises in all World Cup history by sending the Italians packing from Ayresome Park, Middlesbrough, back home to a splodgy welcome from their tomato-wielding fans.

Essentially indeterminable, faraway countries, fielding players with unpronounceable names of whom we know little, often lead the aristocrats into the most embarrassing pratfalls. Italy will not forget the initial jolt which Haiti gave them in 1974 and West Germany will certainly commit the Algerians to memory.

The determination of the underdog – Kim Jung-nam of South Korea

Group therapy as South Korea qualify

South Korea themselves are likely to prove the most unpredictable package of the so-called minnows among this year's entrants. Unlike many of their predecessors they did not unerringly clobber all comers in their Asian qualifying group – their best effort was slotting four goals past the Nepali goalkeeper in Seoul. They even lost a game in Malaysia.

National team manager Kim Jung-nam has cast the basis of a sound defence, the mark of any successful minnow in the World Cup finals – even the energetic Cameroons had a reliable backline. In their eight qualifying games the South Koreans let in just three goals.

This is a rare achievement, for Kim has had his problems moulding together a disciplined unit. In addition to the bulk of his players who come from professional clubs, he has recruited several from the 1988 Olympic team, including Kim Jong-boo, Kim Sam-soo and No Soo-jin. Club football is more adventurous and Kim's success in curbing excesses is a major reason why South Korea will take their place in Mexico.

The manager admits his team produces its best soccer on the counter-attack, as proved in their well-worked victories over Japan in particular. So if shocks are in store in the Cuahtemoc stadium in Puebla and the Olympic '68 stadium in the Mexican capital then it is the pedantic Europeans who should show some anxiety. Bulgaria, and possibly even the Italians, are likely candidates to come a cropper.

It is perhaps unfortunate for the Asians that their opening tussle of the tournament is against Argentina who, of their three first-round opponents, might be considered the likeliest to give them a hiding. Much more is expected of the 1978 champions this time around after their costive displays in Spain.

The Koreans impressed during their Latin American tour at the turn of the year. Mexico only managed a 2–1 victory and the Asians turned the tables on fancied minnows Algeria and won by two clear goals. Yet most anticipate that goalscoring will be their major problem in the finals themselves.

If the South Koreans are to breach the opposing defences with significant penetration then much could depend upon the availability of their top striker Cha Bum-keun, who plays for Bayer Leverkusen in the West German Bundesliga. Cha, because he plays club football in Europe, did not feature in any of South Korea's qualifying matches.

Cha's Bundesliga commitments have already interfered with South Korean manager Kim's careful and intensive preparations for Mexico and at one point Kim was pronouncing himself '. . . not sure that the addition of Cha will help reinforce the power of the team.' But the manager relented by the end of last year and added Cha to the squad.

Underneath the statements, seemingly made for public relations purposes, there is a hint that rivalry exists between the home-based players and Cha, who has made good away from home.

Full-time soccer is still embryonic south of the 38th Parallel. Though it has now become the most popular sport in South Korea, the first professional club – Halleluyah – was established only six years ago. Even so, the Korea Football Association was still hoping to host the 1994 Cup finals after their nation's successful bid for the Olympic Games in 1988.

One of the current top clubs is Pohang Iron and Steel which supplies two of the national team's more prominent players, full-back Chung Yong-hwan and Choi Soon-ho.

Chung, 25, is at his best coming forward and combines well with the front men. It was he who set the Koreans on their way to Mexico in the away leg of the East Asian zonal final in Japan with a powerful strike from outside the penalty area. His club colleague Choi created the winner in their 2–1 victory by dribbling half the length of the field before laying the ball off to midfielder Lee Tae-ho of the Daewoo club to score from close range.

The goals and the performance typified the Korean tactical style of cat-and-mouse play. So it was not a surprise when they failed to enhance their superiority over the Japanese emphatically in the second leg, taking more than an hour to break down the visitors' defence for the one and only time.

That strategy has been underlined in a rigorous, and maybe over-demanding, preparation for the finals themselves. Manager Kim put his players' stamina to the test for a full six months. They began with a two-month tour of Latin America at the end of last year. Then he exerted them for two months from February building up their physical strength with warm-up matches against other finalists. And then after a break at the beginning of April there was a 20-game final warm-up.

It is the sort of intensive scheme which could easily backfire and leave the players burned out before they take to the baking-hot stadiums of Mexico. But if Kim has produced a team to shock the world, then the fruit-sellers of Buenos Aires, Rome and Sofia will be rubbing their hands with anticipation.

SVETLANA'S BOYS COULD MAKE IT EDUARD'S HAPPIEST BIRTHDAY

DERYK BROWN

It was a Russian guide who first gave Deryk Brown the idea that her compatriots were agreeably sceptical about the national team. Here he reminisces about a trip to Russia, and wonders how they will fare in Mexico . . .

She was called Svetlana, and she liked her history, especially her Ivan the Third. We had been touring the Kremlin for an hour when she delivered one of her party pieces. 'We have seen the Tsar's cannon,' she chirped. 'It was cast in the sixteenth century but has never been fired. We have also seen the Tsar's bell. That weighs 200 tons and has never been rung. And there is a third wonder of the Russian world, our national football team. That travels the globe but never scores a goal.' And Svetlana smiled Slavonically.

A few days later I saw Dinamo Kiev play at home. They beat Ararat Erevan 2–0 before a crowd of about 70,000. The Ukrainians gave a lovely, loose-limbed display despite the sapping heat. It occurred to me – as it must have done to many Western soccer buffs – that if only the Soviets could put an act together, they could surprise the world. Alas, 15 years later, I am still waiting.

If I hadn't lost the programme for that Kiev–Ararat match, I could have checked whether Oleg Blokhin was playing. He would have been starting his career about then. Whether he will still be pursuing it (internationally, that is) in Mexico in the summer of 1986 is uncertain. He will be 33, therefore not impossibly old. But his speed, inherited from his mother, the Ukraine's leading sprinter of the late forties, cannot be what it was. He is no longer an out-and-out striker. But that biting left foot still works well enough, and in August 1985 Blokhin became the first man to score 200 goals in the Soviet championship.

Blokhin, however, failed in Spain four years ago. After the USSR lost their opening World Cup qualifying match in Dublin in September 1984, he was dropped. He had acquired the reputation of being a moaner when the going got tough, and his display against the Irish had, apparently, annoyed his colleagues. That looked like the end for Golden Oleg, European

The Soviet superstar, Oleg Blokhin

Rinat Dasayev (Soviet Union), one of the outstanding goalkeepers of the finals

Footballer of the Year in 1975, and the only Soviet apart from Lev Yashin to gain that honour. But a year after Dublin, Blokhin was recalled for a friendly against Romania in Moscow, which the USSR won 2–0. Then he played in two of the three home matches – against Denmark, Ireland and Norway – which completed the USSR's qualifying programme. But by then a rival for the number eleven shirt was emerging: Georgi Kondratiev, an up-and-coming striker with Dinamo Minsk. He has the pace of a young Blokhin.

A young man who is being more directly compared with Blokhin is another Oleg, Oleg Protasov, a 22-year-old striker with Dnepropetrovsk Dnepr, adept with both his head and his feet. If they are true to type, the Soviets will field only two forward players in Mexico; Protasov seems certain to be one of them. England followers may remember him from the USSR side which won comfortably by 2–0 at Wembley in June 1984. Then a rookie international, he scored the second goal.

Forecasting Soviet football long-term can be as tricky as studying blank Politburo faces during a Red Square parade. However, others from that

The Soviet Union's Alexander Chivadze

Fyodor Cherenkov of the Soviet Union caught doing a runner

Wembley line-up are likely starters in Mexico, chiefly Rinat Dasayev, the goalkeeper who some believe is better than Peter Shilton, and who is the most talked about Soviet player; Alexander Chivadze, an experienced hand, who is a free-moving sweeper; Anatoly Demyanenko, an attacking full-back (who, incidentally, the Russian-speaking Tony Galvin tormented in Dublin); and Sergei Aleinikov, a midfielder who lines up with Kondratiev for Dinamo Minsk.

The Soviet team was written down, written off even, after that opening defeat in Dublin. The simple fact was, however, that four of their first five qualifying matches were away from Mother Russia. In August 1985 they played friendly warm-up matches in Moscow against Romania (Blokhin's recall) and West Germany, and they won them both without conceding a goal. They did not concede a goal either in beating Denmark, Ireland and Norway, with Fyodr Cherenkov of Moscow Spartak (another man for Mexico) running the midfield on the first two occasions. When Norway came to Moscow, the USSR needed only a draw to make sure of their Mexico place. They won, Kondratiev scoring the only goal.

So, when the World Cup follows the Olympic Games to the Soviet Union, put your last rouble on the home team getting to the final, if not winning. Meanwhile, Soviet excursions onto the world stage tend to end in disappointment, if not recrimination. Even the great Yashin confesses that he was mortified when an inexperienced journalist reported back from Chile in 1962 that he was to blame for the team's failure. 'I nearly retired,' wrote Yashin, 'but I came to my senses in time, and lived the offence down.'

Dasayev, Yashin's modern-day counterpart, wrote in his book *The Team Begins With the Goalie,* that after Spain both Blokhin and Ramaz Shengeliya returned home 'to the most severe sounding'. 'Oleg flared up at training sessions and at the games. He blew his top over any trifling matter. . .Ramaz, a very sensitive and vulnerable man, became as modest and gentle on the field as he is off it. . .' So it is not only English soccer stars who get as sick as parrots.

It is, of course, wrong to blame two players, however eminent, for a World Cup failure, and after Spain, the Soviet coach Konstantin Beskov lost his job. His successor Valery Lobanovsky went the same way after the USSR failed to qualify for the European Championships of 1984. Eduard Malofeyev came next. He played for the USSR when they achieved their best result in the World Cup, fourth place in England in 1966. With Dinamo Minsk he was first a schemer-goalscorer, later an outstanding coach. He is young for the international stage. He will be 44 on 10 June, the day after the USSR complete their three Group C matches in Mexico: against Hungary (in Irapuato), against France (in León), and against Canada (Irapuato again). If the Soviets have not reached the second stage, poor Eduard might as well set fire to his birthday cake and eat the candles. Defeat will not go down well back home.

The Soviets should survive Group C, although their preparation is sometimes questionable. In 1982 they arrived in Spain only the day before they faced Brazil. (They lost 2–1 after leading and looking good, their one defeat during that World Cup.) When they came to England in 1984 they were in and out in just over 48 hours, hardly the way to permeate the international scene. And any feeling of isolation must be heightened by the fact that the Soviets always travel away without supporters.

Back at the Kremlin, young Svetlana had been too sceptical about a Soviet side which was soon, in 1972, to come runners-up to West Germany in the European Championship. But, very probably, the average Muscovite and the average Londoner is fairly sceptical about his national side. Both are more used to failure than success; both have feted their goalkeepers down the years but have often cursed their forwards (England, too, dried up in Spain when it mattered); and both probably expect that in Mexico their team will fall to the Latins sooner or later.

We shall see. The Soviet camp should have learnt a lot by now. Perhaps this will be the year they will surprise us all. And if Golden Oleg Blokhin, now approaching his 100th cap, can, as a swansong, make a few more goalkeepers hop about, so much the better.

Eduard Malofeev, the manager with Soviet hopes riding on him

PAST GLORIES MEAN NOTHING TO FRANZ

COLIN MALAM

For the first time that most people can remember, West Germany do not necessarily go into the finals of a World Cup as one of the favourites to win it. They are included among the top six seeds in Mexico but that privileged position was, at the turn of the year, based more on past glories than on recent form. Colin Malam of the Sunday Telegraph *wonders if things are really as bad as they seem.*

By the end of 1985, a run of six matches without a win (their worst sequence of results since the War) hardly seemed to equip West Germany for survival, let alone success, in the company of Uruguay, Denmark and Scotland, their opponents in the most fiendish first-round group to have emerged from the December draw.

But, of course, writing off West Germany has never been the most sensible or rewarding of occupations. They have appeared to be in disarray before (notably in 1974, when they won the World Cup despite rumours of internal strife) only to regroup and display that overpowering sense of unity and purpose which has always characterised their most effective work.

World Cups do tend to have a stimulating effect on them, as well. This will be their ninth successive appearance in the finals since they were readmitted to FIFA following the Second World War and began competing again in 1954. Only the ever-present Brazil can match that record of consistency.

Indeed, a World Cup now without West Germany would be like Egypt without the Pyramids, television without Wogan, gin without the tonic: in other words, just about unthinkable. Once in the finals, too, they don't mess about. Twice winners of the trophy, they have also finished as runners-up on two occasions.

It cannot be too much of a hindrance, either, to have as a manager this time a man who is perhaps the finest footballer ever to have played for West Germany. A man, moreover, who appeared memorably in the finals of the 1970 World Cup and has direct personal experience, therefore, of Mexico's unusually taxing heat and altitude.

Strictly speaking, Franz Beckenbauer should not be called West Germany's manager. Because he does not hold one of the precious coaching licences issued by the Deutscher Fussball-Bund – the West German FA – the handsome, elegant, 40-year-old former midfield player or libero is entitled to call himself only 'team chief'. In fact, his appointment in 1984 broke just about all the rules.

For nearly 50 years, West Germany's method of appointing their national team manager had never varied. The job was passed down by the departing incumbent to his assistant with all the regularity and solemnity of a royal line of succession. The system did not fall far short of 'The King is dead. Long live the King!' and all that jazz.

First there was Dr Otto Nerz, founder of the dynasty. He resigned in response to Germany's 2–0 defeat by unrated Norway at the 1936 Olympics – Hitler's Games – and was succeeded by his assistant, Sepp Herberger. The latter reigned for 28 years, during which he made his country, now West Germany, world champions against all the odds in 1954.

Herberger also took West Germany to the semi-finals of the World Cup in 1958 and to the quarter-finals in 1962 before retiring in 1964 at the age of 67. As was by now the custom, Herberger gave way to his assistant, Helmut

Rivetting viewing: Franz Beckenbauer and Co. on the bench watch West Germany lose 3–1

Schoen, under whom the West Germans enjoyed their greatest success in international football.

Runners-up to England in the 1966 World Cup, they reached the semi-finals in Mexico four years later, and then won the trophy in West Germany in 1984. Schoen eventually retired after the 1978 World Cup finals, the only ones in which his team did not distinguish itself. Naturally enough, the new manager proved to be Jupp Derwall, Schoen's assistant.

The continuity and stability offered by the West German practice of allowing the national team manager to groom his successor had been the envy of the world. So the unexpected decision to bring in Beckenbauer from outside the magic circle after Derwall had failed to impress was a measure of the seriousness of the situation in which West German football suddenly found itself.

By the standards of most countries, Derwall had not done half badly. Under his guidance, the West Germans won the 1980 European Championship and finished as runners-up to Italy in the 1982 World Cup. But a disappointingly feeble defence of the European crown in 1984 and obvious disaffection between him and leading members of the national squad led to crisis point and the manager's resignation at the second attempt.

Since Beckenbauer's contract is for two years only, there can be little doubt that, initially at least, his appointment was seen as an experiment, a short-term boost to a flagging team. According to the most popular theory, Beckenbauer was simply holding the fort until Helmut Benthaus had fulfilled his contractual obligations as coach to the Stuttgart club.

But as Benthaus said at the time: 'Who knows what can happen in a year or two?' And for a year at least, it looked as though 'Der Kaiser', as he is known affectionately the world over, would make an imperial go of the job.

West Germany began their World Cup qualifying campaign quietly enough. A predictable 2–0 home win against Sweden was followed by a plodding, 3–2 victory in Malta. But it burst into blazing life with a 2–1 away win against Portugal, semi-finalists in the 1984 European Championship, and an even better one (5–1) in Czechoslovakia on May Day, 1985.

It was after that things started to go wrong. Having had to wait until the Bundesliga programme had finished, the West German squad arrived in Mexico City only a few days before a summer mini-tournament and were punished heavily for their lack of acclimatisation. Their foretaste of Mexican conditions consisted of two defeats. They lost 3–0 to England and 2–0 to Mexico.

Beckenbauer put on a brave face about the outcome of fixtures to which he had been committed by others. He acknowledged the risk West Germany had taken by arriving so late, but insisted it was worth it for the players to experience at first hand Mexico City's exhausting heat and thin, polluted air.

He could also console himself with the thought that his squad had been weakened substantially by injuries and the demands of the Italian Cup, which deprived West Germany of Rummenigge and Briegel – a bigger blow to them, arguably, than the loss of Hateley, Wilkins and Francis was to England.

Rummenigge and Briegel were missing again because of club commitments with Inter-Milan and Verona when West Germany lost 1–0 to the USSR in Moscow last August, a time when the Soviet players were at the height of their season but the West Germans were just beginning theirs. Even so, Beckenbauer was not satisfied with the performance.

He was happier about his team's display in their next match, a 2–2 World Cup qualifying draw in Sweden. The one point was all West Germany needed to qualify for Mexico, and their manager felt they had played very well for an hour, during which they built up a 2–0 lead.

But then the roof fell in. Playing Portugal at home last October, West Germany lost their proud record of never having been beaten in a World Cup qualifying tie. Further humiliation was only narrowly avoided a month later. The West Germans appeared to be heading for another qualifying defeat at home when Czechoslovakia led 2–1 with three minutes to go. But Rummenigge managed to squeeze home an equaliser which took him past Uwe Seeler's total of 43 international goals. (The West German captain still has some way to go to get near Gerd Muller's record 68, though.)

Beckenbauer forgave his players those lapses on the grounds that,

Spain '82: Bryan Robson (England) and Paul Breitner (W.Germany) become temporarily Siamesed. Germany skipper Karl-Heinz Rummenigge considers how to disentangle them

Beware of the keeper: Harald Schumacher (West Germany)

Spain '82: Pierre Littbarski races away in the W. Germany v France semi-final won by W. Germany on penalties

A possible transformer – West Germany's Bernd Schuster

West Germany's wily veteran Uli Stielike

subconsciously, they had probably relaxed after qualifying. He took the view that they had played well when they had to win, and was equally philosophical about the criticism that followed this miserable run of four defeats and two draws.

'We have not played well since qualifying,' he agreed, 'and people have a right to complain.' Equally candid and realistic was his assessment of West Germany's current ranking in world football: 'Brazil, Argentina, France and Italy are technically better than us at the moment. We come next, with Russia and Denmark.'

Having experimented on a large scale both tactically and in the selection of players, Beckenbauer was intending to use this year's fixtures leading up to the World Cup finals as an opportunity to stabilise the side. 'I've never played the same team twice,' he confessed. 'That's because of injuries and loss of form as well as the experiments. But the time for experimenting has come to an end. Now I must find a settled team.'

Although West Germany are as short of outstanding individuals as most other countries these days, there is a solid nucleus of talent and experience around which their team chief can build. Schumacher, Karl-Heinz Forster, Briegel, Rummenigge and Littbarski, for instance, remain from the side that lost 3–1 to Italy in the final of the 1982 World Cup.

If he feels he needs even more experience, Beckenbauer could also call on the wily, versatile Ulrich Stielike, whose influence in midfield has obviously had something to do with the progress of Xamax Neuchatel, the Swiss side for whom he now plays, in the UEFA Cup this season.

To that old guard, Beckenbauer is expected to add players like midfield man Mattäus, defenders Herget, Brehme and Berthold and, provided he recovers from serious injury in time, striker Rudi Völler, all of whom have proved themselves genuine international material since the last World Cup. There are high hopes, too, that 19-year-old midfielder Olaf Thon will realise his potential in Mexico.

But the one player West Germany need more than any other appears to be beyond their reach. Bernd Schuster, Barcelona's gifted midfield artist, could transform them into possible winners of the World Cup. This temperamental star has refused to play for his country so often, however, that Beckenbauer has resolved never to ask him again.

It remains to be seen whether the obduracy of the exiled prima donna and the resolve of his angry national team boss can withstand, on the one hand, the dazzling publicity given to the World Cup finals and, on the other, any continuation of West Germany's poor form.

With or without Schuster, the West Germans will have a struggle to qualify from their tough opening group. Once into the second, knock-out stage, though, anything could happen. As Dr Wilfried Gerhardt, the charming, helpful and knowledgeable secretary of the DFB says: 'Perhaps it's a good thing for a change not to go into a World Cup as one of the favourites: it takes the pressure off. And, in the finals, we do tend to improve as we go along.'

HOW THEY QUALIFIED

MEXICO
(qualify as hosts)
ITALY
(qualify as holders)
BRAZIL
(winners, South American group 3)

Bolivia	2-0	(a)
Paraguay	2-0	(a)
Paraguay	1-1	(h)
Bolivia	1-1	(h)

WEST GERMANY
(winners, European group 2)

Sweden	2-0	(h)
Malta	3-2	(a)
Portugal	2-1	(a)
Malta	6-0	(h)
Czechoslovakia	5-1	(a)
Sweden	2-2	(a)
Portugal	0-1	(h)
Czechoslovakia	2-2	(h)

FRANCE
(winners, European group 4)

Luxembourg	4-0	(a)
Bulgaria	1-0	(h)
East Germany	2-0	(h)
Yugoslavia	0-0	(a)
Bulgaria	0-2	(a)
E. Germany	0-2	(a)
Luxembourg	6-0	(h)
Yugoslavia	2-0	(h)

POLAND
(winners, European group 1)

Greece	3-1	(h)
Albania	2-2	(h)
Belgium	0-2	(a)
Greece	4-1	(a)
Albania	1-0	(a)
Belgium	0-0	(h)

ARGENTINA
(winners, South American group 1)

Venezuela	3-2	(a)
Columbia	3-1	(a)
Venezuela	3-0	(h)
Columbia	1-0	(h)
Peru	0-1	(a)
Peru	2-2	(h)

URUGUAY
(winners, South American group 2)

Ecuador	2-1	(h)
Chile	0-2	(a)
Ecuador	2-0	(a)
Chile	2-1	(h)

ENGLAND
(winners, European group 3)

Finland	5-0	(h)
Turkey	8-0	(a)
N. Ireland	1-0	(a)
Romania	0-0	(a)
Finland	1-1	(a)
Romania	1-1	(h)
Turkey	5-0	(h)
N. Ireland	0-0	(h)

NORTHERN IRELAND
(runners-up, European group 3)

Finland	0-1	(a)
Romania	3-2	(h)
Finland	2-1	(h)
England	0-1	(h)
Turkey	2-0	(h)
Turkey	0-0	(a)
Romania	1-0	(a)
England	0-0	(a)

SOVIET UNION
(runners-up, European group 6)

Republic of Ireland	0-1	(a)
Norway	1-1	(a)
Switzerland	2-2	(a)
Switzerland	4-0	(h)
Denmark	2-4	(a)
Denmark	1-0	(h)
Republic of Ireland	2-0	(h)
Norway	1-0	(h)

SPAIN
(winners, European group 7)

Wales	3-0	(h)
Scotland	1-3	(a)
Scotland	1-0	(h)
Wales	0-3	(a)
Iceland	2-1	(a)
Iceland	2-1	(h)

DENMARK
(winners, European group 6)

Norway	1-0	(h)
Switzerland	0-1	(a)
Republic of Ireland	3-0	(h)
Soviet Union	4-2	(h)
Soviet Union	0-1	(a)
Switzerland	0-0	(h)
Norway	5-1	(a)
Republic of Ireland	4-1	(a)

SCOTLAND
(runners-up, European group 7)

Iceland	3-0	(h)
Spain	3-1	(h)
Spain	0-1	(a)
Wales	0-1	(h)
Iceland	1-0	(a)
Wales	1-1	(a)

(winners, play-off v Oceania champions)

Australia	2-0	(h)
Australia	0-0	(a)

HUNGARY
(winners, European group 5)

Austria	3-1	(h)
The Netherlands	2-1	(a)
Cyprus	2-1	(a)
Cyprus	2-0	(h)
Austria	3-0	(a)
The Netherlands	0-1	(h)

PORTUGAL
(runners-up, European group 2)

Sweden	1-0	(a)
Czechoslovakia	2-1	(h)
Sweden	1-3	(h)
Malta	3-1	(a)
West Germany	1-2	(h)
Czechoslovakia	0-1	(a)
Malta	3-2	(h)
West Germany	1-0	(a)

BELGIUM
(runners-up, European group 1)

Albania	3-1	(h)
Greece	0-0	(a)
Albania	0-2	(a)
Greece	2-0	(h)
Poland	2-0	(h)
Poland	0-0	(a)

(winners, European play-off)

The Netherlands	1-0	(h)
The Netherlands	1-2	(a)

(on away goals)

BULGARIA
(runners-up, European group 4)

Yugoslavia	0-0	(a)
France	0-1	(a)
Luxembourg	4-0	(h)
East Germany	1-0	(h)
France	2-0	(h)
Yugoslavia	2-1	(h)
Luxembourg	3-1	(a)
East Germany	1-2	(a)

PARAGUAY
(runners-up, South American group 3)

Bolivia	1-1	(a)
Bolivia	3-0	(h)
Brazil	0-2	(h)
Brazil	1-1	(a)

(winners, South American play-offs)

Colombia	3-0	(h)
Colombia	1-2	(a)
Chile	3-0	(h)
Chile	2-2	(a)

CANADA
(winners, CONCACAF group 3)

Haiti	2-0	(h)
Guatemala	2-1	(h)
Guatemala	1-1	(a)
Haiti	2-0	(a)

(winners, CONCACAF play-offs)

Costa Rica	1-1	(h)
Honduras	1-0	(a)
Costa Rica	0-0	(a)
Honduras	2-1	(h)

IRAQ
(winners, Asian group 1, sub group B)
Jordan	3-2	(a)
Qatar	0-3	(a)
Jordan	2-0	(h)
Qatar	2-1	(h)

(winners, Asian second round)
UAE	3-2	(a)
UAE	1-2	(h)

(on away goals)
(winners, Asian play-offs)
Syria	0-0	(a)
Syria	3-1	(h)

SOUTH KOREA
(winners, Asian group 3, sub group A)
Nepal	2-0	(a)
Malaysia	0-1	(a)
Nepal	4-0	(h)
Malaysia	2-0	(h)

(winners, Asian second round)
Indonesia	2-0	(h)
Indonesia	4-1	(a)

(winners, Asian play-offs)
Japan	2-1	(a)
Japan	1-0	(h)

ALGERIA
(bye, African first round)
(winners, African second round)
Angola	0-0	(a)
Angola	3-2	(h)

(winners, African third round)
Zambia	2-0	(h)
Zambia	1-0	(a)

(winners, African play-offs)
Tunisia	4-1	(a)
Tunisia	3-0	(h)

MOROCCO
(winners, African first round)
Sierra Leone	1-0	(a)
Sierra Leone	4-0	(h)

(winners, African second round)
Malawi	2-0	(h)
Malawi	0-0	(a)

(winners, African third round)
Egypt	0-0	(a)
Egypt	2-0	(h)

(winners, African play-offs)
Libya	3-0	(h)
ibya	0-1	(a)

FINAL EUROPEAN TABLES

Group one
	P	W	D	L	F	A	Pts
Poland	6	3	2	1	10	6	8
Belgium	6	3	2	1	7	3	8
Albania	6	1	2	3	6	9	4
Greece	6	1	2	3	5	10	4

Group two
	P	W	D	L	F	A	Pts
West Germany	8	5	2	1	22	9	12
Portugal	8	5	0	3	12	10	10
Sweden	8	4	1	3	14	9	9
Czechoslovakia	8	3	2	3	11	12	8
Malta	8	0	1	7	6	25	1

Group three
	P	W	D	L	F	A	Pts
England	8	4	4	0	21	2	12
N. Ireland	8	4	2	2	8	5	10
Romania	8	3	3	2	12	7	9
Finland	8	3	2	3	7	12	8
Turkey	8	0	1	7	2	24	1

Group four
	P	W	D	L	F	A	Pts
France	8	5	1	2	15	4	11
Bulgaria	8	5	1	2	13	5	11
E. Germany	8	5	0	3	16	9	10
Yugoslavia	8	3	2	3	7	8	8
Luxembourg	8	0	0	8	2	27	0

Group five
	P	W	D	L	F	A	Pts
Hungary	6	5	0	1	12	4	10
The Netherlands	6	3	1	2	11	5	7
Austria	6	3	1	2	9	8	7
Cyprus	6	0	0	6	3	18	0

Group six
	P	W	D	L	F	A	Pts
Denmark	8	5	1	2	17	6	11
Soviet Union	8	4	2	2	13	8	10
Switzerland	8	2	4	2	5	10	8
Rep Ireland	8	2	2	4	5	10	6
Norway	8	1	3	4	4	10	5

Group seven
	P	W	D	L	F	A	Pts
Spain	6	4	0	2	9	8	8
Scotland	6	3	1	2	8	4	7
Wales	6	3	1	2	7	6	7
Iceland	6	1	0	5	4	10	2

Above: Caught in mid-flight. Tony Woodcock buzzes Finland goalie Olli Huttunen as the ball runs free

Right: Maybe Bryan Robson's celebrating the fact that someone else besides him can score goals for England. Tony Woodcock (hidden) scrambles the second against the Finns

Below left: Pauno Kymalainen and Olli Huttunen sample the Wembley grass as Tony Woodcock leads the England charge

Below right: It's not like this in Italy. Mark Hateley enjoys a wide berth from the Finnish defence

Goalie Yassar gives his own chances the thumbs down as Tony Woodcock keeps the pressure up

Bryan Robson rises high to put England on the way with goal number one

N.IRELAND v ENGLAND 0–1

We can't go on meeting like this. England and N. Ireland tangle with themselves and each other

ROMANIA v ENGLAND 0–0

Two hands are better than one head. Romanian goalie Silviu Lung punches clear from Gary Lineker

Look, three hands. England stalwart Terry Butcher unravels himself for a high ball

Keep your heads down, here comes Viv Anderson

Grace and power – Francis and Kymalainen

Stefenescou of Romania and Lineker of England lead the chase

The ball that got away. Goalmouth action as England hunt for victory

A solo performance from Chris Waddle

ENGLAND v N.IRELAND 0–0

Four studies in genius. Pat Jennings frame-by-frame as he makes a vital save from Gary Lineker

ROMANIA v N.IRELAND 0–1

Now get after that. Norman Whiteside tells the Romanians where to go in Bucharest

Alan McDonald beats the Romanians for height as Steve Penney looks on anxiously

Above: Not one of his Bett efforts ... Scotland's Jim Bett has the Iceland defence on its knees, only to dispatch his shot over the bar

Right: It takes two – Icelandic defenders Thrainsson and Bergs find they need to work in tandem to stop Alex McLeish

SCOTLAND v SPAIN 3–1

Above: Paul McStay glides past Spain's Urtubi

*Right: It's all done with wires. Graeme Souness
appears to be giving Spain's Victor an uplifting
experience*

*Below: Captain Graeme Souness stops his opponents
in their tracks*

SPAIN v SCOTLAND 1–0

Opposite page: Aerial ballet as Francisco Clos of Spain loses out to Alex McLeish and Willie Miller

Right: I tell you, he was this much offside....Paul McStay gets the better of Spain's Gallego

Below: Spain's Roberto doesn't have it all his own way. Alex McLeish flies in to challenge

SCOTLAND v WALES 0–1

Above: Kevin Ratcliffe looks as if he's spent better evenings as Mo Johnston keeps his distance

Right: Diving for the finishing tape? Ian Rush beats Willie Miller and Co. in the race to the ball

ICELAND v SCOTLAND 0–1

Right: A brief but painful encounter. Roy Aitken clashes with Eggert Gudmundssen while Richard Gough looks on

Opposite page: Steve Archibald makes a grab for the sky as Saevar Jonsson goes in for the tackle

Above: Bottoms up as Steve Nicol of Scotland and David Phillips of Wales head off in different directions

Left: Move over, we're not at Everton now. Club colleagues Pat Van Den Hauwe (Wales) and Graeme Sharp (Scotland) find themselves on opposite sides for once

Below: He's all yours. The referee appears to be giving Scotland's Richard Gough carte blanche rather than carte jaune as he chases after Mark Hughes

SCOTLAND v AUSTRALIA 2–0

One of Dalglish's dodgier moments
Charlie Yankos keeps his hands to himself as Frank McAvennie charges through

Gordon Strachan cracks a tough nut

Above: Maurice Malpas tries walking on air as a way to get round Australian defender Alan Davidson

Right: Roy Aitken fights for elbow room against the Australian defence

Below: Australia's Robert Dunn hitches an uninvited piggy-back ride on Frank McAvennie

FOLLOWING IN THE FOOTSTEPS OF THE CLASS OF '70

BOB HARRIS

If France depend heavily on the incomparable talents of three times European Footballer of the Year Michel Platini, Poland on the pace and proven goalscoring ability of Boniek, Argentina on the inspirational qualities of Diego Maradona, then England can rightfully point towards Bryan Robson as the key figure in their Mexican challenge. Bob Harris talks to the captain behind England's progress to the World Cup.

No slur is intended on Robson's talented England team-mates, for there is no doubt that Bobby Robson's bid is based on the squad system rather than individuals; but his importance to both club and country have been underlined when he has been missing and, unfortunately, he has been absent from a good many games for Manchester United and England. The injuries have ranged from broken legs to a dislocated collar bone and they have kept him out of World Cup ties and a domestic Cup final.

Critics and England-bashers have been quick to seize upon these absences to prove that he is particularly prone to injury and, amid much shaking of heads, maintain that, even if he is able to lead England in Mexico, the intense heat of Monterrey or the altitude of Mexico City will eventually lay him low. Robson treats the comments with the contempt they deserve. His bones are no more brittle nor his muscles less developed than any other professional footballer – it is just that Bryan Robson is a lot braver than most and many of his worst disabilities have come when he has chased lost causes or stepped over that fine dividing line between bravery and stupidity.

Indeed, if strength and fitness are to be a critical factor in the Mexico World Cup finals, then Robson will have a head start on most. He proved this last summer on England's close season trip to Mexico City and Los Angeles. Robson adapted to the unusual conditions as well if not better than most. 'Those preparations last year are going to be a telling factor,' confirmed the England captain. 'We will go out to Mexico knowing exactly what we have to face in terms of heat and altitude and, given the right length of time to prepare, we will be better equipped than most.

The incomparable Bryan Robson, getting in some experience at the Aztec Stadium, Mexico City

'We all learned a great deal on that trip, not least of all that there is nothing to frighten us in the conditions, particularly over the altitude and the hazard with food. In all the time we were away last year there was only one case of stomach ache and that came about because one of our senior players drank too much orange juice. By contrast the Germans arrived late and within a couple of days half of their squad were in serious trouble.

'Bobby Robson and his staff, particularly our doctor Vernon Edwards, got it absolutely spot on and we all have the confidence that they will do it again. The biggest problem we will face initially will be the heat. I am told it is regularly $100°$ in the shade and this can take its toll. But we faced exactly the same problem during the last World Cup finals in Spain when we played France in stifling heat in a concrete bowl in Bilbao. We found it tough but the French found it even tougher. We beat them 3–1 and they were considered by many to be the best team in Spain!

'One of the reasons we survived better than our opponents was again due to the right preparations. The doctor had done his homework and we ate the right food, drank the right amount of liquid, took our salt tablets and brought our temperatures down with cold towels at half-time. We coped then and we will cope this time.

'As for myself I pride myself on my stamina which I have built up over the years. I am well aware of my capabilities; I am making no plans to change my style just because a lot of people who have never laced on a pair of football boots say that only those who pace themselves can survive. I believe I can slow a game down when necessary but I also believe that I can run any marker into the ground.

'It will be exactly the same conditions and difficulties for the players of Poland, Portugal and Morocco because there are few countries who play their football in the heat of the day. A feature of games in Portugal, for example, is the lateness of their kick-off times, often nine or ten o'clock. We are also fortunate that all three of our games are at the later start time of 4pm; that must be a lot easier than the noon kick-offs which are designed to cater for television rather than the poor footballers who will have to suffer the consequences.'

There are no complaints either from Robson over the opposition in the opening round, and the only question raised – and then taken completely out of context – was over playing at near sea-level at the start of the tournament and then having to move up to altitude against teams who would be acclimatised to the extra demands.

That is why Bobby Robson went straight from the draw to Monterrey to scout out a suitable training camp in the Sierra Madre mountains before settling on a luxury hotel in the University town of Saltillo some five and a half thousand feet above the industrial city where England will play all three of their matches in Group F. Before that England will live and train at altitude in Colorado Springs in the US. In between, Bobby Robson and Dr Edwards will have talked to everyone who can contribute a sensible thought or theory on the right build-up.

'Let's face it,' said Bryan Robson, 'there are no easy games in a World Cup finals; if that sounds like a cliché then just look through some past results, particularly since the competition has been opened up to take in the Third World teams. We will be taking Morocco every bit as seriously as Poland and Portugal. But we will be looking to win our group for the privilege of staying in Monterrey for the second round when some other team will have to come to us and get used to the difficult conditions in far less time than we will have had to get ready.

'One look at Scotland's group with West Germany, Uruguay and Denmark and we have to be pleased with the draw we were given, especially with a minimum of two and, in some cases, three teams progressing to the knock-out stage of the competition.'

There is no doubt that a fit, healthy Bryan Robson can use the massive stage of the World Cup finals to lift himself into the higher echelons, right there alongside the likes of Platini and Maradona. His qualities are different but the end product can be the same with match-winning goals and defence-splitting passes. Where Robson can triumph, even against his illustrious rivals, is in his enthusiasm and leadership. Too often, Platini and Maradona flare up because those around them have not had the vision or the ability to achieve what their captain has demanded. Robson will just go harder and encourage more.

As there have been question marks over his fitness, there have also been those who have doubted his leadership qualities. Even Bobby Robson and Ron Atkinson had Bryan's great friend Ray Wilkins ahead of him as skipper initially. Maybe in the early days he was a little too quiet, far too concerned with getting his own house in order rather than telling others what to do. But no longer. Bryan Robson not only leads by example but also in the best traditions of captaincy. Other players respect his ability and also discover that they can relate to him because he is so down to earth and unchanged by the sort of lifestyle that has been known to turn more than one footballer's head.

Born in the little village of Witton Gilbert just north of Durham, he has all the characteristics of the Geordie with no time at all for pretensions and falsehoods. His father Brian was a long distance lorry driver and it meant that Bryan, sister Sue and brothers Justin and Gary had to pull their weight around the house to help their 'mam' Maureen. It was not the environment for breeding swollen heads and neither was the Black Country of the West Midlands where he learned to ply his trade with unfashionable West Bromwich Albion.

He showed an abundance of talent in those early days but it was not only the austere surroundings of smoking chimneys and slag heaps which kept his feet on the ground. He broke his left leg twice and his right leg once in the space of seven months, the third time against Manchester City just a few days after being selected to represent his country in the Under 21 side. Maybe it was because his career was so close to a premature conclusion in the ambulance on the way to hospital that he can now appreciate what he has achieved and ridicule newspaper talk that he was finished this season because of a pulled hamstring and a strained calf muscle.

Home life has also followed a similar pattern. Sitting with him in the ambulance on that third occasion was his fiancée Denise and his mother Maureen. Denise has been a constant source of inspiration to him just as his mother and father were during his early days. It takes a very special, thoughtful bride to welcome the groom home from a club tour of Denmark on Friday, wed on Saturday and then see him go off on an England Under 21 tour the very next day. Denise is not even that keen on football!

It could have changed dramatically when Bryan moved from the homely surroundings of the Hawthorns to the demands of Manchester United at Old Trafford, particularly when the move provided a British record transfer fee of £1,750,000 and even more so when the giants of Italian football waved bundles of banknotes his way in a bid to prise him from United. With some considerable encouragement from Ron Atkinson, his manager at both Albion and United, he resisted the temptation and signed a long-term, rewarding contract for Manchester United.

He has old-fashioned values about matters like loyalty, family and team spirit and they all blur the edges between his private life with his wife and daughters and his highly public professional life. He can be objectively critical about United or England, but never to outsiders; when he is away from his family he gathers his team-mates around him like a second overcoat, encouraging them to do things together, whether it is going to a bar or restaurant at the end of a tour or to the cinema in the middle of one.

He has managed to bridge that important gap whereby he has the ear of the manager without losing his close connections with his fellow players. He is even closer to his team-mates than Kevin Keegan, who enjoyed being one of the boys but was always recognised as the super star. In the end it rebounded on England and Keegan in Spain, for the former European

Bryan Robson practises holding the FIFA World Cup (actually it's a replica but a man must have his dreams)

The family connection: Bryan Robson with Denise and daughters

Footballer of the Year was unfit until the final stages and then expected to step straight back into the team. Manager Ron Greenwood compromised by putting Keegan on the bench for the critical game against hosts Spain; although Keegan came on he missed a great opportunity and the vibrations, bad before the game, were even worse afterwards.

Bryan Robson admitted: 'It was catch-22 for our manager Ron Greenwood. Should he keep an unchanged team or bring back Keegan and Trevor Brooking, neither of whom had played a single game? Kevin knew in his heart that the game against Spain was his last chance of World Cup glory and he was bitterly disappointed that he did not start.

'We needed to win that game by two clear goals to stay in the competition but, as we did against West Germany, we drew 0–0 with Spain and went out, with the Germans going forward to the semi-finals to meet France because they had beaten the Spaniards 2–1.

'It was a cruel way to finish the competition for we had won three, drawn two and lost none, conceding only one goal and that against France. Although we had gone further than many people thought, we were distraught for we knew we were capable of going the distance.

'The current squad is, if anything, even better. We may not have a star like Kevin but we have the depth and that is going to be an important factor in the heat and altitude of Mexico. There is no way the same eleven players will be able to play right through a tournament of this nature. We will need everyone.'

Robson made a spectacular start to the 1982 World Cup finals – in fact the best ever! He scored two of the three goals against the popular French, the first after 27 seconds, the fastest goal ever scored in a World Cup tie; Steve Coppell took a quick throw, Terry Butcher back-headed and Robson, timing his run to perfection, stretched out his left leg to score from an awkward height. Soler equalised but Robson hurled himself full length to head in a cross from Trevor Francis for the second.

The man in action: a typically agile moment of excellence as Robson shoots past Jean Luc Ettori of France in Spain '82 to score the fastest goal ever recorded in the World Cup finals – just 27 seconds after kick-off

I felt then that we were going to be hailing Robson as a true giant of world football at the end of the tournament, but the injury jinx struck again when he limped off against Czechoslovakia and missed the dull 1–0 win over Kuwait. Although he fought his injury without moan or complaint and came back to play against the Germans and Spain, he was never 100 per cent and that, to me, was the difference between England's success and failure. At that stage of the tournament Robson and Steve Coppell had become even more important than Keegan and Brooking, and while the attention focused on the latter's selection it was the absence of Coppell and the missing gear of Robson which blunted England's goal threat.

It was while in Bilbao that Bryan Robson became a father. Not only had he left Denise behind a day after their wedding, football duty took him away at just the wrong moment for the birth of daughter Charlotte. Bryan was not in the best frame of mind as he battled the injury in the knowledge that there was a momentous event happening in the West Midlands. It helped slightly when his father-in-law telephoned to tell him that all had gone well and that mother and daughter were fine; later that day his spirit improved when he was able to speak to Denise on the telephone ... but it was going to be such a long time before he could see his new-born baby.

He did his best to put it out of his mind as he drank a celebratory glass of rioja with the squad over dinner and then prepared to do yet more television for the folk back home. He settled down in front of the screen expecting to comment on some World Cup action when, to his surprise and amazement, his wife and daughter appeared on the screen, filmed earlier that day in hospital by the friendly Midlands television crew.

In the four years that have elapsed since then Bryan Robson has grown in stature as a player, a person and a captain. Fitness permitting, he will make his mark. His tigerish tackling, his raking passes and those late, surging runs which carry him into opponents' penalty areas at the optimum moment make him not only an exciting player to watch but also a match winner for England.

'That is what counts,' he said, 'not individual performances. Our game has gone through an awful period and I believe every player in the squad is fully aware of the responsibility he shoulders. Success for England would give the game at home an enormous lift and bring spectators back to the turnstiles as well as repairing our damaged prestige abroad.

'It is not being over-optimistic to suggest that we can succeed, for there is not an outstanding team in the world at the moment. You can never undervalue teams like Brazil, France, Argentina and, the best of the outsiders, Denmark. But I honestly think that this is the best England squad since the 1970 finals in Mexico.'

If that is indeed true then the armchair viewers at home are in for something special, for Alf Ramsey's defending champions were truly world class and, but for the illness that afflicted Gordon Banks and Ramsey's disastrous late substitutions, England might well have retained the World Cup. If the class of '86 can match what happened until then...

ENGLAND'S FIRM FOUNDATION

RONALD ATKIN

What makes Peter Shilton, at 36, the world's best goalkeeper?
Shilton talks to Ronald Atkin, of The Observer, *about the attitude,*
the determination and the mental strength needed to stay at the top.

If you believe in building from a solid base, as every good team manager should, there's no firmer foundation in football than Peter Shilton. Bobby Robson readily acknowledges the fortune he, and England, possess in this respect – indeed, he practically has to be anchored to the floor as he enthuses about the England goalkeeper.

Shilton will be nearing his 37th birthday when England compete in Mexico, but the man's extraordinary combination of ambition and dedication ensures there is no likelihood of his being dislodged from the summit just yet.

Lev Yashin, one of the greats, in action for the Soviet Union

The goalkeeping art: Italy's veteran Dino Zoff in the 1982 final against W.Germany

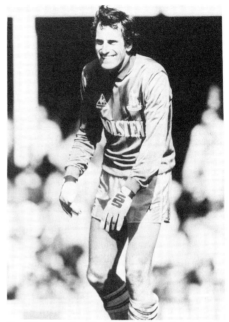

The ball looks like an extension of Pat Jennings's hand as he prepares to throw

Ray Clemence, the other half of some good-natured rivalry for the England jersey

Great keepers like Lev Yashin, Dino Zoff and Pat Jennings extended their careers beyond 40 and Shilton intends to match, perhaps even exceed, these legendary names. In 1985 he signed a new contract with Southampton which will take him into his 40th year and, having passed Gordon Banks's record number of 73 England caps in the World Cup qualifier against Turkey at Wembley last October, Shilton is firmly embarked in pursuit of Jennings's (still growing) world record of international appearances.

Shilts, as he is known to his friends and playing contemporaries, would by now certainly have progressed far beyond the century mark but for the fact that his career has paralleled that of Ray Clemence. Of Robson's predecessors as England manager, Don Revie preferred Clemence, while Ron Greenwood resolved an inability to make up his mind about who was the better by alternating them.

Robson, however, was in no doubt from the moment he took over the England job after the 1982 World Cup. Shilton's was the first name on the team sheet. 'Shilts is the best goalkeeper in the world,' says Robson, 'because of his stature, his presence, his professionalism and his appetite for work, quite apart from his ability.

'Since I came on the scene as a player in the fifties there has been nobody better. He looks so big in goal that from ten yards out you wonder how you can ever get the ball past him. Not only does he make saves between the posts, not only does he dominate his penalty area but he also controls the first 30 yards of the pitch and commands his defence. Who else has done all that?

'Apart from being a great goalkeeper Shilts is a wonderful motivator and a great talker. He demands respect and gets reaction from the other players. Apart from doing his own job he also works for the people in front of him. He is terrific, the best, in that aspect of it. Nor has he ever lacked courage, which is essential to a goalkeeper. If you are playing in the Maracana in front of 200,000 people and you're a bit afraid, go and stand next to Shilts.

'Despite being in his mid-thirties his reactions and reflexes are excellent and he is really a dedicated trainer, a maniac. He trains harder than anybody I've ever seen and there's no reason why he shouldn't retain his agility and body condition for another five years.'

Shilton agrees with that last estimate. 'I feel I can go on for a lot longer. I think it's ambition, really. I like to think I have always been pretty dedicated.'

That dedication dates back to the days when he used to hang, sandbags tied round his ankles, from the banisters of his parents' home in Leicester, trying to grow tall enough to become a goalkeeper. He claims, 'It's still a pleasure to me, not work, to stay fit, though I'm no longer quite so fanatical about it. Youngsters should do everything they can, in every spare moment, to increase strength of muscle and joints but when, like me, you're playing two matches a week for eleven months a year you have to stick to a normal routine basically.'

Peter Shilton at an England training session in Helsinki, May '85

Since what Shilton terms a normal routine would certainly demolish lesser men, it's worth recording in some detail his thoughts on fitness and some of his specialised routines.

'Goalkeeping requires a different type of fitness to outfield players, so obviously it's a specialised type of training. In goalkeeping there are so many things you have to be spot on with and if you aren't quite right in just one of those things it shows up all your other good work. For instance, an outfield player can be one-footed and it still doesn't prevent him being good but one weak thing will always let a goalkeeper down. It's an old saying but true that you are judged on your mistakes. In that respect goalkeepers are in an extremely vulnerable position.

'Basic agility work helps keep the body supple – getting up and down quickly, adjusting your body weight from one point to another. Then there are the footwork exercises. A goalkeeper is a little bit like a boxer in this respect, or even an American footballer. You have to have quick feet and be able to use them in a confined area, taking as many short strides as possible.

'While outfield players concentrate on 60-yard sprints we are operating on speed of reaction by moving from side to side between fixed cones. We also have half a dozen balls spread out in a ten-yard radius and, starting from a certain point, you have to touch each ball, going back to the starting point each time.

'A goalkeeper has to be strong but agile, supple not stiff, and he needs quick reaction of eyes and hands, in a short space and repeatedly. I have developed what I call a 'triangle routine' to help my reflexes. I am in a small goal, three or four yards wide. On one side of that goal, to the left or right, stands a server, who throws the ball about knee height to a striker in the centre of goal about six or eight yards out and he volleys it at you. So it's serve-volley-keeper.

'If it's done right that's the hardest exercise I do because you have to get your feet out of the way quickly, moving in every direction as you react to the shot. You are literally like a rubber ball bouncing around in that little goal. The idea about not making the goal too big is that you aren't at full stretch all the time, just saving balls a yard or two either side of you.

'A variation on this is to have the same small goal with me facing the back of the net and a striker standing eight yards out. I throw the ball between my legs and turn. By then the ball should be on its way back, sometimes low, sometimes high, sometimes straight at me, sometimes wide of me.

'Then there is long shooting practice, saving shots from the edge of the box and a bit further out. There are so many different angles involved that this could be a full session on its own, if need be. I am experienced enough now to know if I shouldn't have been beaten from a certain angle in a match, or if I haven't punched a couple of balls properly, so I do something about it in training.

'You can also practise standing on the penalty spot, having balls chipped over the top of the defence and sprinting outside the box to kick them away, in other words playing as a sweeper.

'Finally, you come to your crosses. Like shooting practice, there are so many different angles the ball can come in from, short or deep. This will be one of the most important things in Mexico. At altitude the ball moves a lot quicker. Once you are in position for a shot, even if the ball flies more quickly, you are more or less at the right angle to deal with it whereas on crosses you have to give yourself enough time to adjust your options.

'Obviously goalkeepers work together a lot in training, but we also like to join in with the other lads. You can get a bit isolated otherwise. So maybe you join in the odd five-a-side or run around with them and have a sweat.'

It was in a five-a-side practice on an all-weather pitch that Shilton incurred one of his rare injuries, a pulled muscle, just before Christmas. While he was recovering he took his wife Sue and sons Michael and Sam to a pantomime. 'When we came out of the theatre it was raining, so I ran to

The Shiltons at home: Sue, Peter, Sam and Michael

the car and the muscle went again,' he said, thus proving that even the most dedicated of athletes are not immune from such freak injury.

As well as being a stickler for training Shilton insists on the right form of relaxation. 'When I have trained hard I need to make sure I get the proper sort of rest. Sometimes resting can be the hardest thing in football. When you have come off the training pitch absolutely shattered it takes you until the next morning to recover. You don't have the mental energy to do anything else and it's important as you get older to make sure you recover properly.'

A confirmed DIY duffer and non-helper around the house, Shilton puts his feet up at home, watches TV in a non-demanding fashion, takes the dog for a walk or ambles around the golf course. Strangely, he also finds it easier to relax before a match than afterwards, which is why, he says, Sunday is 'a bit of a strange day, because I always feel mentally and physically tired, even as a goalkeeper. It's a difficult day because I've got two active lads and they want me to go out and play cricket and football. I try to do it as much as I can, but they are beginning to realise now why I sometimes don't feel like it.'

In the matter of diet Shilton says he is a basic eater, though he has only one large meal a day. Breakfast is usually a cup of tea, lunch consists of sandwiches and more tea. 'I like meat and veg and the night before a game I'll have steak, salad and perhaps chips and I usually end up with a rice pudding. I eat as I feel, really. I am at the stage now where sometimes my body will tell me when I need something. I may even occasionally have some Smarties or a Mars bar, especially after matches. Basically my diet is a balanced one but if I am really hungry I will treat myself. I work and train hard so I never have any weight problems.'

Shilton is also a master at the art of relaxing before a game. 'Of course you have to be physically sharp but you also have to be mentally right,' he says. 'It isn't enough to do your training and think you will be okay, you must be mentally ready, knowing you will concentrate 100 per cent throughout the match and give everything you've got. That means you have to want to look forward to the game.'

When he stops looking forward to a game and when he stops caring about a goal going past him – in other words when his performance falls below his own demanding standard – Shilton says he will know before anyone else that it is time to retire. But until that moment he is anticipating with relish the World Cup as a member of an England squad he considers the best he has ever played with.

'We had a very good basic team in the 1982 World Cup and all we failed to do was score goals at the right time. Now we have a bit more quality, especially in terms of strikers, so I'm looking forward to a good competition.'

Everyone, except those with the thankless task of putting the ball past him, will share Peter Shilton's hope that England enjoy an even better World Cup than in 1982.

SAMPDORIA SMOOTHIE WITH NOTHING TO LOSE

BOB HARRIS

As a race the Scots have, at times, been guilty of overestimating their own capabilities. That was certainly the case when Ally MacLeod led the 'tartan hordes' to Argentina for the 1978 World Cup finals. Eight years on, Bob Harris talks to Graeme Souness and finds out there is no chance of that happening in Mexico.

The draw in Mexico City last December which pitted Scotland against seeded West Germany, South American champions Uruguay and the tournament's most dangerous floaters, Denmark, left even the most rabid Jocks reaching for the branch water and shaking their heads in dismay. Certainly the reaction of Scotland's captain Graeme Souness was one of disbelief with more than a touch of envy at England's good fortune.

For a sophisticated world-traveller, who faces the best every week in the fiercely competitive Italian League, his instant reaction was a throwback to the back streets of Edinburgh and his immediate response definitely unprintable. Severely censored and with the telephone held at arm's length it sounded something like: 'How unlucky can you get? How can England talk about drawing the short straw in Monterrey when we have to play three of the best teams in the world? Somebody in Mexico must have had it in for the Scots.'

Time has not reduced the awesome task facing Alex Ferguson and his team, but the initial shock has worn off and holidays are no longer being booked for the middle of June. Not that Souness would be tempted into making rash, or even beefed up, predictions after sitting on the bench in embarrassment in Cordoba eight years ago when he watched his team-mates' confidence drained away in a 1–3 defeat by Peru and a 1–1 draw with outsiders Iran. Now he is simply a realist.

'The whole thing in Argentina was a total disaster,' he recalled. 'But in those days I was very much the junior who could only squirm at what was said before we left for Argentina and again while we were there. It was overkill and it rebounded on everyone in those two opening games that we were supposed to win at a canter. It was only when everyone had written us off for our final game against Holland that we showed exactly how well we could play, beating the eventual runners-up 3–2 in Mendoza.

'That was a fine performance and we came desperately close to displacing the Dutch in the competition; but instead of being grateful for escaping with some of our reputation intact, that victory was used as proof that we could have gone all the way in the competition.'

Souness omitted to mention that he was one of the major reasons why the team suddenly discovered its form, emerging from the bench to produce a masterly display that was to point the direction for his future. At the time Souness was also establishing himself at Liverpool where he was to become captain and pile up five Championship medals, four League and Milk Cup final victories and three European Championships. It was all a far cry from those early days when, training with Celtic, he was chased through the streets of Glasgow by a lunatic waving a sword, or even when he was a

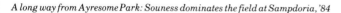

A long way from Ayresome Park: Souness dominates the field at Sampdoria, '84

A shot from the past: Graeme Souness in his
Middlesbrough days, '75

The good life – Danielle and Graeme Souness at home

youngster at Spurs unsuccessfully demanding a first team place and then nipping off home to Scotland when he didn't get what he wanted.

His current team-mates at Sampdoria would find it hard to equate the smooth, clearly wealthy man of the world with the lager-swilling, pot-bellied young athlete who was warned about his future as a professional by manager Jack Charlton at Middlesbrough. But unlike many of his more volatile countrymen he has learned from his mistakes, smoothed off the rough edges and now rightly holds his head high in any company or society.

He has charisma and is undoubtedly a celebrity – in demand by television hosts and always offered the prime table at establishments like Langan's but a desperate disappointment to the Fleet Street gossip columnists. The only 'crimes' he commits are on the football field when his now occasional lapses bring the wrath of football's officialdom down on his head. That sort of stuff is left to the back pages.

'They would have loved me when I was younger,' he laughed. 'But when I was up to all the sorts of thing they would be interested in I meant nothing to them. There have been times in my career when I admit I could have gone off the rails but somehow I saw sense and that, combined with a burning ambition for success, kept me just within bounds.

'Even when I joined Liverpool I could have blown the lot, as I enjoyed the good life and thoroughly earned my nickname of "Champagne Charlie". Two things happened to change all of that. On the pitch our manager Bob Paisley made me captain of Liverpool while off it I met and fell in love with Danny. Both events gave me the sort of responsibility I had never experienced before and I relished and encouraged it.'

What happened on the pitch is history but it all went hand-in-hand with events off it. The marriage to the delightful, blonde Danielle may have been made in heaven but the peripheries could well have come straight from the Stock Exchange. Graeme, by this time, was earning well, with regular bonuses to sugar the cake. It might have all gone the way of so many footballers' cash in an investment in a risky bar or restaurant, but Danny's father Austin is a brilliant businessman and Souness was bright enough to know good advice when he heard it.

Danny came into some of the family wealth via a maturing trust fund and, right on cue, the Genoa-based Sampdoria club stepped in with an offer which not only secured the Souness future but also saved a considerable number of pound notes from finding their way to the Inland Revenue as the family moved out of range. As if to prove it was not just for the money, Souness went on to inspire his new club to their highest-ever league placing (fourth) in the Italian League and to their first-ever triumph in the Italian Cup, a remarkable irony considering the Cup was the one trophy that would never come his way at Liverpool.

The Souness lifestyle now befits his status. He, his wife, daughter and two sons, live in a magnificent apartment in the coastal resort of Nervi, next door to England international team-mate Trevor Francis. The mountains of Switzerland and the beach resorts of the South of France are within easy reach for this jet-setter, while his official residence is on the island of Majorca (another sound investment by father-in-law Austin), with further bricks and mortar in the posh part of North London. Neither he, his wife nor his children need want for much in the foreseeable future and, with a three-year contract tucked under his belt, it would have been the easiest thing in the world to have ambled his way into gentle retirement.

But as much as Graeme Souness loves the lobster and champagne merry-go-round his taste for competition remains undiminished. Nothing about this hard man of football has gone soft and that fact has not gone unnoticed by the managers from England, Italy and Switzerland who have followed his progress; no one has any doubt at all that he will eventually finish up in management as a hard, mean, driving boss.

'There is a great deal of water to go under the bridge yet,' he mused, 'not least of all this World Cup in Mexico. After that . . . who knows? I am quite happy to let other people speculate and if you are to believe all that is written I am going to be playing in such diverse places as Australia, where I was supposed to have bought a house after our World Cup qualifying match, Switzerland, not to mention running and playing for Fulham, being assistant manager to Kenny Dalglish at Liverpool, as well as player-manager at both Arsenal and Spurs. No one knows the truth because I don't know it myself.

'I do want to go into management but it has to be the right club. It need not be a First Division club, but it does need to be one with ambition which will be keen enough to want to win things as badly as I do.

'As a footballer I always wanted the best and I see no reason to change my ways when I do step back over that white line. Scotland? Why not! But I guess that may just have to wait for a while.'

That may not be the joke it was intended to be, for not only has he the apparently obvious qualities to make a successful manager but he has also built a growing store of international knowledge reaped not just from three European Cup triumphs but also from three World Cups. After the débâcle in Argentina, where Souness was one of the few to come away with his reputation enhanced, came Spain and a much saner campaign under the guidance of 'Big Man' Jock Stein. This time there was none of the hysteria of four years earlier.

'We still managed to blow it,' said Souness. 'It was the same old story with the problem coming against the supposed easiest team. It happened in Munich when Scotland scored only twice against Zaire and went out on goal difference although unbeaten.

'It was the same in Argentina. Even after underestimating Peru we should still have taken care of Iran but we could only draw with them. In Spain we beat New Zealand right enough, scoring five goals against them in Malaga but we gave away two and, after losing to Brazil and drawing with Russia, we missed out again.

'I thought that was a difficult group, but what's it like this time? I confess I was very despondent when I first heard the draw in Italy on a Sunday night in December. I had just been sent off by the same referee who had sent me off 12 months earlier and it was all I needed. All I could see was the quality of the opposition. West Germany, who always produce their best at World Cups, Uruguay, who are rated even higher than Brazil – our opponents four years earlier – and the Danes. How can Denmark be classed in the same group as Morocco, Iraq, South Korea, Canada and Algeria? It was a joke to start with and an even sicker one when we drew them.

'It struck me somewhat forcibly that we, Scotland, would go out to Mexico as the underdogs of our group, the least fancied of four teams. It means we go there with nothing to lose and no one tipping us to topple the world. It is a situation Scots relish, back to the wall and all that sort of stuff. There are no soft touches and that may just be to our benefit; we are going to be keyed up for every game. However, I doubt whether any of our opponents will dismiss us lightly.

'They are going to take points off each other and every game in the group is going to be difficult for all the teams, not only Scotland.

'We must have a positive attitude . . . and we will. No predictions, but at least there is a chance of three teams going through and our minimum ambitions must be for one of those places. Otherwise it would not be worth going, would it?'

There is another, unspoken, reason for Souness and his team-mates to do well. The late Jock Stein. Souness had grown close to the 'Big Man' and was as stunned when Jock died in Wales as if it were one of his own family. Souness had been forced to sit that match out for earlier indiscretions against the Welsh at Hampden and away to Iceland, and he was aware that all was not well with his friend when he came down from his seat in the stands at half-time with the Welsh winning 1–0 and Scotland on their way out of the competition.

Stein stayed alive long enough to see his team come back to equalise from the penalty spot. Clearly there were problems but there is little doubt that the tension and excitement of that electric night was a contributory factor and so unnecessary. Scotland had swept all before them in the early stages of the competition, beating Yugoslavia 6–1 in a warm-up before going on to take Iceland 3–0 in Glasgow and group favourites Spain 3–1, then throwing away the advantage with a home defeat by Wales, defeat in Spain and a draw in Iceland.

Souness asserts himself against Spain's Senor

Souness said: 'We all know we have been given a second bite of the cherry and we are grateful for the opportunity. Playing in a World Cup finals is special and we know it. We will go out to Mexico and give our opponents the respect they deserve. God help them if they don't reciprocate.'

SPEEDO'S PLACE IN THE SUN

NIGEL CLARKE

Once upon a time, life for Scotland's David Speedie was mainly about keeping fed and warm. Now he's at Chelsea and his life has been transformed, as he tells Nigel Clarke of the Mirror.

The little Scot would get wearily out of bed, and use a ten pence piece to scrape the frost and hoar off the inside of the bedroom window.

Life for David Speedie five years ago was all about keeping warm.

He was Darlington's star striker, and Number 8, Harcourt Street, a cold, damp, two up and two down terrace house, a far cry from the £120,000 mansion he owns now in the stockbroker belt of Camberley.

But Speedie will never forget those days. That's why he puts himself about the way he does, that's why he's so hungry. He never wants to go back to them.

He was married to Joanne then, and paid £8 a week rent for the accommodation that he says 'was freezing. There was no heating apart from a gas fire downstairs, no garden, just a brick yard where the outside loo used to be.'

The front door opened out directly onto Harcourt Street; in winter Joanne used to go to bed in socks and a cardigan. 'We used to kiss and cuddle a lot to keep warm,' she smiles. She adds: 'In the summer if we wanted to sunbathe, we'd have to go to Butlins.'

All this shaped the character of Speedie, and when Chelsea came in for him with a £65,000 offer he suddenly saw a way out into the big time.

'I've always been a winner,' he says. 'I hate losing, I get the needle if my wife beats me at Scrabble. And I'm sickened if I have to come second. Doesn't matter what it is, golf, anything, but especially football.

'But my life has changed so dramatically, from Darlington to Mexico in five years. Incredible, but there's no way I'll ever take it for granted.'

For Joanne it's more frightening: 'Sometimes I don't know where I am,' she says. 'In five years, we moved to Chelsea, had two children, Charlotte, 3, and David, 15 months, moved into a lovely house in Camberley, and now he's off to Mexico with Scotland. It's hard to take it all in. You sometimes wonder where it's all going to end.'

Speedo the hard man, giving it and taking it for Chelsea

Speedie's nickname at Chelsea is 'Albert', after Albert Tatlock the old moaner of *Coronation Street* fame. He moans at training, rucks everybody even himself. Micky Thomas labelled him, and Speedie swears he'll be looking out for him next time West Brom and Chelsea meet.

The fact is, as a hard man, Speedie gives it and takes it too.

His legs are covered in bruises and abrasions, and there's rarely a Saturday when he's totally free from one knock or another. The spitfire in Speedie will send him plunging in where lesser strikers fear to tread.

'It's my game,' he says. 'No defender likes being put under constant pressure. But when you think of it, I'm still learning. I know I can improve everything about my game. I want to be the best. That's not daft, is it?'

The fact that he's now a marked man amuses him. 'Proves I'm doing my job,' he smiles. He and Kerry Dixon have emerged as perhaps the most lethal partnership in the First Division, and he goes on: 'Every season I set myself targets. Every season so far I've reached them. I should get more goals than I do but, as I improve my game, I believe they'll start to come regularly. Playing with Kerry helps. He's so quick, but I've never met anyone who loves a goal more. He genuinely gets the hump if I score and he doesn't. So we are rivals and friends, but rivals first and foremost within the framework of the team. We both know if we score enough Chelsea are going to end up winning something.'

In the heat of battle: Speedie gives it all he's got as usual

An old-fashioned centre-forward: Kerry Dixon, Speedie's partner in triumphs at Chelsea

A white Ford car sits impressively in the drive of his new home. Down either side is written David Speedie, Chelsea and Scotland, but he's not flash yet, and keeps a low profile about his lifestyle.

'It's got to be different, mate,' he says. 'At Darlington I didn't even have a motor for over a year. I used to hop on the bus, 15 pence fare it was. I always thought that was a take on.

'I used to wonder what it was like being a football star. I wanted to be one so badly. I'd dream about it, and work hard at everything I did.

'It took my breath away when Chelsea came in for me. I didn't know much about them, just that they were a very big London club.'

Speedie put himself about from his very first day there, but when he was dropped at the start of the Second Division promotion campaign, I found him sulking in a Fulham Road restaurant. Chairman Ken Bates had taken

Enjoying the good times: David and Joanne Speedie with Charlotte and David

out all his reserve as a thank you for being the back-up boys to the first team squad. Not even the delights of the meal, and the fact that the chairman was paying, could pick up Speedie's spirits.

'This is no good to me,' he snarled. 'I know Mr Bates means well but I want to be in the first team. If I get back in, I'll tell you something, I won't come out again in a hurry.'

He got in the following week, and hasn't been dropped since, apart from suspensions. 'I'm proud of that,' he goes on. 'The fact is I've never been dropped by any team I've played for. I like to think I give every bit of myself to every game. It's the only way I know how to play.'

That way has got him into trouble, with defenders who want to kick him black and blue, and with referees who are looking for him. He was suspended three times last year, sent off once, and recorded 42 disciplinary points. This year he's been off once, and served one suspension. 'I swear I'm learning,' he says. 'I don't argue back so much now. I just try to get on with the game. But referees don't give you any protection. Defenders take liberties; they can get way with it because they are always facing the ball.'

Speedie is the kind of kid you rub with a cloth and gold dust appears. Chelsea have found that. They rate him at £800,000 and believe he is one of their all-time best-ever buys.

WORLD CUP REFEREES:
A GENUINE LOVE OF THE GAME

TIM WHITBY

*Without a referee, even park football tends to end in acrimony. No
referee means no competitive football. Yet when 36 of the world's best
fly into Mexico this summer, they will receive rather less attention
than the cornflakes the England team will be freighting out to ward
off Montezuma's revenge. It is unlikely that any of them will be
detained in Bogota and accused of stealing a bracelet; and no one
expects to be reading ghosted columns explaining 'My temporary loss
of form: I just can't seem to stick 'em in the back of the book any more'.
The media, and so the public, are simply not interested in
what referees may think or hope or eat for breakfast.
Tim Whitby investigates the phenomenon.*

The World Cup finals have become TV drama and referees play only a
supporting role in this great sporting soap. They are there to see that the
rules are obeyed, but increasingly they have been cast in another role –
that of Ealing Studio Policemen. They provide comic relief to the drama of
the World Cup.

Commentators seldom have much to say about the man in the middle
beyond noting where he comes from: Europe (implying 'serious'), South
America (implying 'corrupt', Asia/Australasia (implying 'inept'). There-
after he is only important when he makes a controversial decision –
preferably an out-and-out howling mistake – or if he is what's known as 'a
character'. This summer, attention is likely to be limited to slow-motion
action replays of refs botching it up: giving 'worked for' penalties (i.e. dives)
or failing to spot a potentially prosecutable tackle.

Some of the 'best' television moments in recent history include the
Egyptian referee, Kandil, who let a Mexican player take a free-kick which
he had clearly awarded to El Salvador (Mexico scored); the Russian,
Stupar, who waved play on when all the Kuwait team believed they'd heard
his whistle – the French duly scored an unopposed goal and Stupar was
faced with the unhappy prospect of the Prince of Kuwait leading his team
out of the competition altogether. And perhaps the best of all was the

decision of Wales' own Clive Thomas to blow the final whistle in the fraction of an instant between a corner connecting with a Brazilian head and the ball hitting the back of the Swedish goal. Such moments as these are deemed worthy of attention.

Mr Thomas also qualified as 'a character'. He was the one with the very hairy legs who used to do a goose step at the kick-offs. Refs don't need to go to such lengths; being bald or, better, fat and out of breath is usually enough. One of the few who made a conspicuous effort was Gordon Hill; he perfected the art of running backwards, smiling and swearing at the same time, but came horribly unstuck handling defenders who themselves did little other than run backwards smiling and could, moreover, swear in many tongues. Other refs, perhaps to overcome the language barrier, have tried adopting either an imposing austere demeanour – short hair and a Messianic stare – or the smiley 'it's only a game lads' face. The trouble is that players know exactly what they are up against and can cheat accordingly.

All this is clearly 'good TV' – anyone making a fool of themselves is generally regarded as 'good TV' – and Mexico 1986 is not likely to be the year that refs are treated any differently. To the man on the terraces, refs are traditionally 'blind, deaf, biased bastards' and the job of the

An almost balletic pose as Clive Thomas arbitrates

More of a military two-step but still in charge

You need to love the game to put up with all this. Munich World Cup referee Jack Taylor sombrely leads a young fan to safety as Spurs and Chelsea fans riot

commentator is to bring that atmosphere into your living room. But while you chortle as a rotund Swedish ref scuttles across the pitch to consult a linesman who only speaks Portuguese, remember that for him this is the climax of a distinguished, and unrewarded, career. As Jack Taylor says, 'referees are only there out of a genuine love of the game.' At the World Cup finals they get a very raw deal indeed.

Getting there at all is extremely difficult. There are about 18,000 registered referees in Britain; the top couple of hundred are on the League list and of these only about a dozen are on the European list. One English referee may be selected by the FIFA Referees Committee, chaired by Harry Cavan, to go to Mexico, but there is no guarantee. FIFA will select from 36 countries whether or not they are participants. Thus, once in Mexico a ref has a 1 in 36 chance of refereeing the World Cup Final itself. This means that it is statistically easier to make the final as a centre-forward than as the man in black.

The apprenticeship itself is cheerfully appalling. Several seasons of non-League football, a few years as a linesman and then the League, perhaps Europe and, as they say, The World – all by the age of 48 (compulsory retirement). If selected by FIFA, it's a minimal-expenses-paid trip to a hotel of their choice, almost certainly sharing a room with another ref. Then it's a three-week 'get together', chatting about the rules, reaching a consensus on 'difficult areas' (like the professional foul or dissent) and training when possible – in Mexico in 1970 some refs were to be found doing early morning calisthenics in parking lots. A ref is guaranteed just one match in charge and maybe a couple as linesman, and on these he is assessed for 'the Big One'. But only so long, of course, as his country isn't in it. In short, once they get to the finals the referees are locked into a private competition to be the man selected for the final itself. Unsurprisingly, therefore, the level of camaraderie is not very high. In Spain, most of those who weren't selected flew home early.

Nor is it a financial bonanza. Although the daily allowance is $100 – more than enough to call home, have a post-match beer, a meal out – there's no compensation for loss of earnings at home, no free tickets, no gifts or souvenirs, no fraternising with the teams, no wives, no free cars and, of course, no 'win bonus'.

FIFA sign sponsorship deals with various sports firms; but while refs are required to wear the official strip, even blow the official whistle and stop the official watch, they personally receive nothing at all. The logic must be that if you do it for the money you are therefore corruptible (like Test Match umpires, I suppose, who receive a considerable salary – last year a basic £7,000 for the six-month season, plus £1,200 per Test Match).

Even when a referee does manage to get onto the pitch and take charge of a match, the World Cup offers peculiar problems. Needle and niggle are a crucial part of the stakes-are-high modern game. Cameras seldom pick up on the clots of phlegmy bile which defenders, like cormorants, are wont to deposit on the nape of opposition forwards ('just to let them know they're there'), the cheery hair-pulling pat on the head (with which full-backs 'apologise' to wingers they have just clattered), or the delicate use of elbow and shoulder to solar plexus and chin (which is generally called 'shielding' the ball). All these tricks, and many more, go on and can theoretically be penalised as 'ungentlemanly conduct', although they seldom are. According to most referees, this is because both sides do it in equal measure, and they prefer to let the game flow.

The challenge of the World Cup is that different nations have a different repertoire of tricks. South Americans aren't used to the European love for tight marking (pushing, pinching and elbowing your man all over the pitch) and hard tackling (crunching, thigh-high fouls), while Europeans object to the 'sly', 'dirty' Latins (the trip, the spit, etc). A European referee will tend to take for granted European 'hard' play, but take exception to South American tricks, and vice versa. It is not surprising that teams can sometimes feel unfairly penalised as a result.

For the players and managers the consequences of success and failure are enormous. Quite apart from the obvious excitement and the enormous rewards of actual victory, the competition has become an international 'shop window'. Players' club careers can be made at the World Cup. They are under great pressure, and that pressure is directly transferred to the referee. Jack Taylor, who took charge of the Germany v Holland final in 1974 in Munich, makes light of such pressure, but it took a very cool man to award a penalty against the Germans before they even touched the ball.

With emotions understandably running high it isn't really surprising that referees become the butt of ridicule or abuse (which of these it is depends, of course, on whether or not the mocker is affected by the decision).

If a game is rough the ref will be blamed for 'losing control'; if it is fair then it is the teams who will be praised for their sportsmanship. Referees can never win.

It is an old football cliché that goalkeepers are crazy: cold, lonely, on a hiding to nothing and with the loss of an ear or finger an accepted occupational hazard. But at least they earn a living and have a chance of glory. The referees who suffer abuse, ridicule and the chance of losing money on a lonely trip abroad do it for honour and a love of the game.

In return for their sacrifices, referees continue to be viewed as comic villains. Television is waiting in ambush for the monstrous gaffe. Then, players, managers, commentators and spectators can unite in their outrage and derision for the man in the middle, the man who is given absolute power to handle the game but who derives absolutely no benefit whatsoever from the exercise of it.

GEORGE COURTNEY

George Courtney is the headmaster of a primary school in County Durham and — in his other profession — one of the most envied people in the world. As a referee, he has been chosen along with 35 international colleagues to take charge in Mexico. He has already reffed 20 internationals worldwide, as well as the finals of the UEFA Cup, Milk Cup and FA Cup. He is married and has lived in the North-East since he was born 44 years ago. His other interests are athletics, reading, golf and people, especially his six-year-old son Matthew.

Q. Did you always want to be a referee?
A. No. I would have loved to have been a player at top level, but they found Bobby Charlton instead. To me, this is just a great substitute.

Q. Have you been to Mexico before?
A. I've not been further south in America than Florida. I did the World Youth Championship in Australia in '81 and the European Youth Championship in Poland in '78, as well as two tours with the North American Soccer League in '78 and '80, which was where I learned to ref in high humidity. Well, that was where I learned to ref, full stop. I went out a callow youth and came back a man, you might say. The games were so bloody tough. All those clashing nationalities and temperaments thrown together. But it was a superb experience.

Q. Talking of clashing nationalities and temperaments, how will 36 people from different countries be able to referee consistently in Mexico?
A. Some of them I've worked with in previous tournaments, like Ramirez the Mexican whom I met at the Asian Championships last year, and it's amazing the camaraderie that exists. But it's up to me. We'll be there eight to ten days before working, all 36 of us, so by the time the first game comes along we'll be in tune. Basically, football's such a simple game that we shouldn't have any problems.

One of a very different breed – England referee George Courtney

Q. Do referees get a raw deal financially?
A. No we don't. We're non-professional in that sense and I suspect the vast majority of referees would do it for nothing. We're a breed apart and we get this kick out of refereeing games, especially at top level, and we're better for being independent. The way I regard it, the headmastering pays the mortgage and the refereeing takes me and my wife out to dinner occasionally.

Q. What do you think the players think of you?
A. I'd hope they thought I was honest, strong, fair, sympathetic and fit. I don't discuss it with them – perhaps I ought to, but we don't get the opportunity of having a natter. We are two very different breeds and I wouldn't want it any other way, but there's nothing I would love to do more than, for instance, go and train with players.

Q. You're known for being an ultra-fit referee. How do you keep that way?
A. My fitness is a result of 30 years of sustained running, squash and regular refereeing. I've got a fairly natural fitness, I don't put weight on. But I also watch what I eat and drink and I've got a big heart and lungs and strong legs, and that's what you need these days. The game has quickened so much in the last five years, and the danger is that referees will be left behind because there isn't any structured training for them. With Mexico, I've got to be as fit as I've ever been. I'm a great

believer in shared pain. I'm always loathe to go out on my own. I have a group of neighbours and friends who go out with me.

Q. As the headmaster of a primary school, with experience in dealing with childish tantrums, do you apply similar methods of keeping order on the football field?
A. I'm spending a third of my life in my teaching job so it must rub off somewhere! No, seriously, I've got to be strong as a headmaster so I'm probably strong on the park. I remember once, four years ago, I reffed Nottingham Forest v Southampton and I cautioned seven and sent one off, and the *Sunday Times* man said he didn't have to look in the programme to know the referee was a headmaster. I've still got that cutting.

Q. How do you cope with the tensions of a game and the abuse of the crowd?
A. Being a fairly extrovert character, I feed off it. If I can break the tension with a smile or a grin I'll try it but only if I've got time. There are games where you can't relax for a minute, but others are more easygoing and you can get a bit of banter going with the crowd, because I think we are sometimes too serious about the game. But I can't respond to orchestrated chants of 'Who's the wanker in the black'.

Q. Do you sometimes feel a game is slipping away from your control?
A. There have been times when I've had to rethink my approach to a player or a game. It can become a bit too easy and that's when it happens. Certainly when I was younger the pressures were greater. It's easier to sell decisions now, make decisions acceptable to players. I look upon myself as a salesman and usually I get good returns.

Q. How do you feel when your game is televised?
A. It gets my adrenalin going. Actually, I have a video library of every televised game I've refereed, and after I get back from a game I'll sit and watch the tape if the cameras have been there. It's important to look and see if I can change my approach or positioning. If it's been a controversial game, it's exacerbated by one's so-called 'friends' in the pub. When there have been no problems in a match, they don't want to know. I suppose they like to see people in high places make a mistake. But pros don't make mistakes.

Q. How do you get your uniform so spruce?
A. Regular ironing by my wife, the power behind the throne! She's quiet and patient and understands the tensions, she doesn't get as involved as me which is a good thing because otherwise I'd drive her round the bend.

Q. Will you referee the final in Mexico?
A. It wouldn't please Bobby Robson if I said yes because that would mean England wouldn't be contesting it. But of course I'd love to do it, I'd be ready for it, they've been preparing me for this. Along with other refs, we've been nurtured for this occasion for years.

Q. The FA has recently been concerned about a growing shortage of match officials. How would you encourage a youngster to become a referee?
A. I'd say, don't be put off. I do a lot of talking to potential referees and I'm telling them the good things about the game. You do go through tough patches and a referee needs a strong character to cope. It doesn't get any easier. But the rewards are there to be had.

THE OTHER SIDE OF THE CAMERA: ITV'S WORLD CUP PLANS FOR MEXICO '86

TOM HARRIS

Go back to a typical Sunday afternoon at the end of the 1960s and a man with a balding pate and a Cheshire cat smile is presenting football on television. A decade and a half later there's a little less hair but the smile's the same and more than eight million fans still share their weekend football with Brian Moore.

This summer, Moore's voice will be as serene as ever when he presents Independent Television's coverage of the World Cup finals but his supremely relaxed style will, as always, conceal furious activity behind the scenes as the ITV team battles against difficulties unique to an international tournament of this importance.

'In Mexico we're going to face filth, pollution and altitude problems,' says producer Jeff Foulser. 'We're going to have to work about 16 hours a day for a whole month. Some of the matches don't start until 11pm our time, so we'll be working until two in the morning some nights. Tiredness starts to

Pastmaster Brian Moore, in commentating action

really hit you after only a week but the adrenalin keeps you going. The crew, like the players, need to have a strong constitution. Last time nearly all of us got ill but then it wasn't so far to fly people home,' he says.

Moore echoes Foulser's sentiments but makes sure he is physically, as well as mentally, prepared for the most gruelling month of his career. 'I find it the most exhilarating month of every four years in terms of my career but I have to be physically strong. I do regular daily exercise and spend a quarter of an hour on an indoor bike every morning. I normally lose half a stone during the finals. It's a tremendous challenge, much like running a marathon. I do get very tired but it really only hits me the month after it's all over.'

In addition, Moore will prepare by travelling to Europe to watch as many of the competing teams as possible before the finals; of the many inevitable advances in technology since the last Mexico World Cup in 1970, he sees the home video as the most crucial for him. 'There is no substitute for getting to know the players and teams that are in the finals and the advent of the video cassette has helped enormously as we can watch them on video now.'

Moore has never covered the World Cup finals abroad, although he did commentate for BBC Radio on the 1966 final between England and West Germany at Wembley, and is likely to lead this year's operation from the London studios. With him will be a panel of football experts to comment on each game and hopefully provide some entertainment.

'We're going to get one whole month of fully peak-time viewing, so people have to respect our panellists and not get tired of them. We've always tried to get people who are extrovert and have popular appeal rather than people who were great World Cup players,' Moore explains.

This year's operation will be similar to the set-up in Spain four years ago with one commentator at each of the six first-round venues and Mexico City used as a headquarters where pictures will be edited and sent to London by satellite. Mexican television will provide pictures for all the world's networks but BBC and ITV will be allowed to set up their own additional cameras when British teams are playing.

'You have to rely on another country's television at the World Cup finals as otherwise there would be 150 cameras and crews at every game,' says Foulser. 'That means the basic quality of the pictures depends on them and, of course, it involves a great expense.

'Mexico is not in a great state financially and it wants to squeeze every last peso out of the world's media. The whole operation will probably cost BBC and ITV together about eight or nine million pounds.'

Some 60 technicians, cameramen, commentators, reporters, and other production staff will go to Mexico, with a staff of 40 based in London. They cannot afford to waste a second as it costs up to £3,000 for the use of satellite for one hour. ITV and BBC work as closely together as possible to ensure the same match is not broadcast live by both channels but competition remains fierce and comes to a climax on final day, the only occasion apart from the FA Cup final when they show the same match simultaneously.

Commentator Martin Tyler   Producer Jeff Foulser

This can mean a few problems for commentators, as ITV's Martin Tyler points out. 'When England are not playing, we often end up in bad positions in the press box. When they are playing, we get virtually pole position but are sometimes so close to the BBC that we can't avoid hearing what each other is saying.'

Tyler sees the six or seven weeks the crew will spend in Mexico as a straightforward matter of survival, something which has to be lived through to be understood. His pigeon Spanish helps, but he admits to the occasional stumble over players' names.

There are occasions, however, when he has been more than grateful for his few Spanish football phrases. In Argentina in 1978 he was so anxious to watch the Argentinians train that he only narrowly avoided a fight.

'You have to be prepared to deal with any of the teams in the finals, even though for the first phase you know which teams you will see,' he says. 'But for the second phase I had to cover the Argentinians, whom I had not seen play. I had heard it was difficult to decipher the numbers on the Argentinians' blue-and-white shirts and they all seemed to have moustaches and long, flowing black hair,' he adds.

But when Tyler tried to enter the ground where the Argentinians were training, he was turned away because manager Cesar Luis Menotti had refused entrance to any members of the media. So Tyler found a convenient fence to peer through and proceeded to watch the training session through a pair of binoculars, until he was confronted by security guards.

'I was a snap of a finger away from getting beaten up. I had to tell them in my pigeon Spanish that I would go home and say I was badly treated in Argentina. It wasn't true, but I was allowed to watch the rest of the training session because they were so afraid of bad publicity,' he says.

Tyler was lucky. The indecipherable numbers were changed before the next match against Poland and centre-forward Mario Kempes shaved off his moustache to try and change his luck in front of goal. The commentator was at an advantage because he was by now familiar with the players.

Although the crew in Mexico will be using Mexican pictures most of the time and broadcasting by satellite, the operation will be based on many years' experience of putting together *The Big Match*. Each week a team of about 45 take their show to a League match in England, while smaller crews are filming second or third support matches elsewhere.

It all begins long before the referee's opening whistle. Commentators have to research the teams involved and prepare a rough script, and 'riggers' spend about six hours wiring up cameras and microphones to outside broadcast lorries. 'Contrary to what many people believe, we normally do *The Big Match* commentary live – it adds immediacy,' says Tyler. 'You can prepare things to say about each player but not for when they score because it can sound false. Like "the bubbles are really blowing round West Ham now". You have to remember people are going to hear what you say over and over again, and it's hard to avoid clichés.'

A commentator can speak almost as loudly as he wishes and need not worry about competing against the crowd because of the equipment used and continually monitored during the match by the crew. Most important is the compressor, which equalises the microphone so that the commentator can shout without seeming too loud. 'Without the compressor, it would be like coming up to your ear and whispering, then shouting,' explains sound mixer Paul Farraday. 'We like to have the crowd very loud for *The Big Match* and Brian Moore likes to be almost drowned out. The match must be exciting and he likes to fight the noise.'

The programme director sits in the scanner, the largest of four outside broadcast lorries, with the match taking shape on a dozen or so screens in front of him. The largest of these shows him which camera is being recorded to appear on the programme. By the flick of a switch, the director selects which camera angle suits each moment of the game. At times it becomes tense in the scanner, as a camera suddenly flickers and dies and pressure mounts. But with plenty of action close-ups, combined with players' grunts as they reach for the ball, the match is sure to be exciting.

The crew's work does not end at the final whistle, for a script must be written, the match must be edited and the programme must be recorded.

Rehearsal time is limited but the team is packed with experience. Director Ted Ayling has been with *The Big Match* eight years and Moore twice as long. He was co-presenter of the programme with Jimmy Hill, who now presents BBC's *Match of the Day,* when it was first screened in 1968.

While the last problems are smoothed over and the programme is squeezed into its alloted running time of about 45 minutes, Moore even finds time to browse through the morning newspapers. It all has the air of having been done hundreds of times.

So this summer when Moore is calmly beaming that beautiful smile while the world's top footballers are pouring sweat in the Mexico sunshine, spare a thought for the backroom boys on the other side of the camera. As Moore says, he can afford to smile because the most important advance for him since the Mexico finals in 1970 is the reliability of his back-up team.

ARCHIE TO TAKE ON THE WORLD IN STYLE

DAVID STEWART

One of Scotland's most distinguished performers is a one-time headmaster and current rector of sorts, who won't even be seen on the pitch – Archie McPherson does his stuff down the microphone. David Stewart talks to BBC Scotland's favourite commentator about his coat and other more vital matters.

Archie McPherson is a difficult man to ignore. From the high-speed hyperbole of his football commentaries to his multi-decibel sports jackets he rarely does anything quietly. But his distinctive red thatch, cleverly disguised as a rusty Brillo pad, is probably his most arresting feature. Dispatched from just above the ear and sent scudding across his shiny dome, its essential fragility tends to be somewhat exposed in the raging gales which seem to lash Scottish football stadiums every Saturday afternoon around five o'clock. The bold McPherson's subsequent attempts to corral his mane can provide even more distracting entertainment than his occasionally light-hearted round-up.

However, it is not just the hairstyle, but the commentary which marks the avuncular Archie out from the babel of his contemporaries. The bland repetition of the facile facts and figures is not a significant part of his verbal repertoire.

'Statistics I suppose are necessary, but they're not really something I bother about too much,' he says. 'Although when I do use them people appear to take more notice.

'For example, in last year's Scottish Cup final I mentioned that if Celtic winger David Provan scored from the direct free-kick he was lining up, it would only be the second time in the history of the competition that it had happened. Of course, seconds later Provan had the ball in the net.

'John Motson was on the phone the next day giving me some stick about it

The BBC's Archie McPherson, a difficult man to ignore

and he was a bit surprised when I told him the local librarian had given me the information when I was handing some books back.'

His preference for comment, and a swift interpretation of the action, can however (given his passion for the game) result in his heart short-circuiting his brain. Perhaps the most famous example of this was at Anfield in 1977 when Kenny Dalglish steered Scotland onto the ill-fated road to Argentina, once again at the expense of the Welsh.

'I undoubtedly went over the top on that occasion, but it was more from relief than anything else. I'm now trying to tone things down.'

Any Scot who can still feel the lump in his throat when he hears Archie's emotionally-charged commentary, matched with those memorable pictures, will regard this as a disappointing development.

'It's a natural progression for me,' he explains. 'Having almost sole responsibility for Scotland's weekly programme of edited highlights over the past two years has helped. I'm now trying to comment on the game as a whole rather than becoming too involved. I want to stand back a bit.'

This carefully nurtured impartiality will be put to the test during the World Cup. Archie has been pencilled in to line up alongside John Motson and the rest, to broadcast nationwide. That means that the days of dual commentary to satisfy xenophobic audiences are over. England could get

McPherson, Scotland could have Motson, depending on the spin of a microphone. Whether or not Archie's new vocal delivery stands up to the pressure of significant Scottish success in Mexico remains to be seen, but his idiosyncratic sense of style is unlikely to be affected.

Unfortunately, the outrageously proportioned overcoat, which gives the impression that he is doing his job while being savaged by a wild animal of indeterminate species, will not be returning to the continent of its origin. The jacket which has brightened up many dull Saturdays for the armchair fan is not suitable for the Mexican climate.

'Believe it or not, that coat is worth a fortune, but I bought it in Peru for £20,' says Archie with the kind of pride in frugality that only the Scots can muster. 'It's pure alpaca, incredibly warm, and would cost anything in the region of £250–£500 in London.'

Archie the celebrity has come a long way from Archie the young headmaster who began his broadcasting career in the sixties by reading a description of his school's nativity play on BBC Radio.

Gradually he worked his way into sport and, most important, football, although he has difficulty remembering exactly when he reported his first match. But puffing ruminatively on an outsize cigar and indulging in a few suitably Castroish gestures it all comes back to him. 'It was at the time of the Cuban missile crisis. I was at Douglas Park, Hamilton, the Accies were playing East Fife, and I was probably the only one in the world who felt that Armageddon would be a welcome relief from what I was watching.'

That acerbity, as well as getting him noticed, has also caused a few problems. 'After my appearance on *Football Focus* with Freddie Starr and Stan Boardman on Grand National day I became regarded as something of a comedian.' Not that he minds that in itself, but he does object to being thought of as a comedian and nothing else.

'There's a balance to be achieved between humour and serious comment. If it's done properly it can be entertaining and informative at the same time. But it's not easy.'

Having convinced the BBC that they have a priceless gem stashed away, Archie is now adding some much-needed sparkle to the hitherto straitlaced football programme. He has also brightened up one of Scotland's most respected academic institutions. As Rector of Edinburgh University, Archie is at the centre of all its decisions. His popularity, it seems, knows no bounds. Following such luminaries as David Steel and Magnus Magnusson he was elected to the position earlier this year topping the poll in all five rounds of the proportional representation voting system.

'Education is very important to me,' says this ex-headmaster. 'Giving up three days a week, and most of my spare time, to work at the university is I think ample indication of that.'

It seems that everybody wants a piece of Scotland's most colourful communicator. English, Welsh and Irish football fans will get their ration in June, and if his past impact is anything to go by they will probably clamour for more.

SOCCERSPEAK: FOOTBALL, IN OTHER WORDS

SUE COX

Confused by what the experts mean when they start talking in Soccerspeak? Sue Cox uncovers the mysteries of the game and offers a linguistic guide.

'I turned on the TV,' said a non-footballing friend, 'and this man with mad, haunted eyes was talking about a sweeper. I thought he meant the old bloke who used to come and do our roads before the government cuts, but it turned out he was a football manager discussing the World Cup. What on earth did he *mean?*'

At four-year intervals, there comes a month of sport which for outsiders must rank as utter hell. By outsiders, of course, I mean anyone so bereft of patriotic fervour, and so unmoved by the delights of sitting in the lounge with the blinds down wondering why Jimmy Hill's chin looks exactly the same with or without a beard, that he or she actually dares to utter sentiments like 'World Cup! Pshaw!' or its modern but unprintable equivalent.

To these joyless party-poopers, four weeks of televised soccer must sound as comprehensible as *Crossroads* performed in Walloon. The reason is that anyone who last saw a game of football in the days when Bobby Charlton could part his hair at a higher level than the corner of his mouth will discover that the lingo has changed unrecognisably.

In the old days, the only agent a footballer had was the chap who used to collect his pools coupon on Thursdays. Players had quaintly self-explanatory names like 'centre-forward' and 'outside-right', not 'sweeper' or 'target man' or 'overlapping full-back', which sounds like a description of his figure after Christmas, not his function on the field of play.

In those days, too, 'man-to-man marking' was something tattooist did to client, there were no television commentators to bamboozle you with impressive-sounding but (on mature reflection) totally meaningless analyses of a perfectly simple free-kick, and no new-wave sports hacks fresh out of Oxbridge who describe eleven men and a ball in words of five syllables. In fact, understanding the rules and expressions of the game required no more than the sort of basic intellectual competence necessary to put your underwear on the right way round in the mornings.

But nowadays a football match is no place for the uninitiated. It's as though you've strayed into a Brueghel painting, a foreign town cluttered with mysterious figures who set their stalls out and sweep up at the back. These characters also have battles at the bottom of the table, a bit like 4B at my grammar school who were the delinquent year and graduated from merely flinging bits of potato at each other at lunch into full-scale drug abuse and organised crime.

Utilising part cliché, part code, a contemporary manager giving a pre-match interview slings together the arcane and the truistic with the brio of a cook trying to resuscitate last night's stew with Yugoslav Riesling. 'This one's a real six-pointer,' he intones of a League match, 'but there's eleven of us and eleven of them and football's a funny game. We've got one or two things up our sleeves and as long as we play for 90 minutes and keep a clean sheet at the back we should be there or thereabouts at the final whistle.' (As a location, 'there or thereabouts' is a matter of faith rather than a fact of geography, rather like heaven or Atlantis.)

A manager of an unfancied side, when interviewed before a game, will invariably state, 'We've come to play football,' which is a terrific reassurance to those of us who thought they were about to indulge in 90 minutes of incest or Morris dancing. When interviewed *after* the game, the same manager will probably say, 'The team showed great character out there,' which presumably means they did Harold Wilson impressions, or dressed up as Mickey Mouse. Incidentally, when such a manager singles someone out as 'one of the game's great characters', it means the player in question is either 1) toothless; 2) feckless, unable to pass a dog track without going AWOL for three days; 3) the genial life-and-soul-of-the-dressing-room type till he gets within 25 yards of an opposing centre-forward, when he turns into a raving killer with bloodshot eyes; 4) wearing a headband.

When this manager refers to the 'great team spirit' in his club, this merely indicates that they can all share the same dressing room without fighting. Such a manager will usually say of football, 'It's a man's game,' thus lifting the shroud of ignorance from all those who thought it was played by Airedale terriers or Yeti. The team he manages will often consist of 'a good blend of youth and experience', or in other words half a dozen haven't yet started shaving, four of them are held together in various places by bits of metal plate, and the goalkeeper's just qualified for Meals on Wheels. It is also possible that he will be celebrating his nomination as Manager of the Month. In days gone by, of course, managers used to keep their jobs a little longer than that.

As well as insecurity of tenure amongst managers, modern football also features 'zonal defence', a subject upon which the experts harp as though it were something desirable like 'personal freshness'. Teams don't win matches any more, they 'get a result', and they aren't called footballers, they're known as The Lads. If they're a 'really great bunch of lads' (i.e. ones who not only share the same dressing room without fighting but actually stand back to let their mate have first go at the blow-dryer) they no longer try hard – they give 110 per cent, which presumably means they give 100 per cent plus a cut for their agents (see above).

When conversing in the new Soccerspeak, players (or Lads) will generally refer to their manager as 'The Boss' or very occasionally 'The Big Man', though never as 'Pratface' or 'Old Droopy-Drawers', unless they want to be given a 'transfer'. (Which, by the way, is nothing to do with those cute pictures of Donald Duck and Goofy you used to soak in water then stick on Granny's Sheraton escritoire when you were a kid.)

Like acne scars, some expressions are always with us. Even those whose participation in sport petered out around the time they found it chipped their nail varnish will dimly remember dragging hockey sticks around school playing fields while huge, red games mistresses thundered alongside bawling, 'Dribble, girl, dribble!' Footballers still dribble. Indeed, caught in full, glorious colour by the omnipresent eye of the TV camera, some do more than that. When Sir Stanley Matthews was called the 'Wizard of the Dribble' he could have had no idea that this term would come to denote the player who could spit the furthest.

Talking about nasty habits, what about 'handling?' The innocent might be forgiven for thinking that that's just one more step down the road of permissiveness now that The Lads need only the provocation of a goal to start snogging with each other. Do not assume, by the way, that the place reserved for that sort of activity is the 'touchline'; a game can get 'physical' anywhere on the field, especially when they're 'keeping it tight at the back'.

Since Ted Heath took us into the Common Market, all sorts of foreign muck seems to have crept into the game. In the past, if you used the word 'catenaccio', everyone would think you were talking about one of the more baroque items on offer at Toni's ice-cream stall outside the ground and serve you right if you were sick after eating it – a 'Throw-up'. A 'Throw-in', on the other hand, has developed into a bit of a free-for-all these days – toilet rolls, coins, beer cans, bottle rings, seats, bits of the electronic scoreboard and, presumably, if your team is 5–0 down with a minute to go, The Towel.

Incidentally, The Towel should not be confused with The Sponge, a magic device used by trainers to revive seemingly moribund players who've been in their last throes just long enough for the referee to penalise the opposing side. (Could that be a Throe-in?)

Since the TV companies have invested large amounts of money in order to beam the World Cup direct from Mexico into your living room, they clearly have to justify the expenditure. The chaps with the key to the TV Centre's executive toilet are not going to be happy if a man with a face like an air crash looms up on the screen and says, 'If you want my advice you'll watch the Doris Day movie on the other channel because all we've got for you is two cruddy teams of dagos drawing 0–0.' No, the commentator has to *sell*. And as for the sports hack enjoying an all-expenses-paid stay in the same hotel as his national side, he's hardly likely to dismiss the centre-forward as a limp-wristed moron if he's going to be eating breakfast at the very next table every morning for the coming month.

Here, then, in order that the public at large can understand to the full the lingo of soccer as spoken on the TV and written in the papers, is a glossary of terms.

An unforgettable game
A mildly eventful game

Played in an exemplary spirit
Both teams indifferent to result

Don't be misled by the fact that this game
was a goalless draw. It was packed with incident
*The keeper had two whole shots to save before half-time
and five minutes from the end a dog ran onto the pitch*

A sportsmanlike game
Stopped short of fatal injury to any of the participants

A committed performance
*Most of the team could actually remember which side they
were playing against*

Controversial
Adjective describing any game with a penalty in it

Dramatic
Any game with a missed penalty in it

Thrilling
Any game with a missed penalty in it and *a goal*

Classic
*Ditto, but with all the action in the last five minutes,
and a dog running onto the pitch*

Ding-dong
Noise made by bell

A solid performance
As in 'X gave a solid performance.'
Boring, but didn't actually do anything disastrous

A promising debut
Shot wide and buried his head in his hands a lot

A quiet debut
I wasn't aware he was on the pitch till I read the programme at half-time

An ambassador for the game
Sometimes wears his team blazer, doesn't spit on-camera

Gentle giant
*Big cretinous defender with his head held on by bolts
who hasn't yet been done for manslaughter*

World-class defender
*Has managed to play for England six times without
putting through his own goal*

One of the game's elder statesmen
*Bald, dodgy knee, sometimes appears on TV with Bob Wilson
and Lawrie McMenemy*

Ballwinner
Small, snaggle-toothed thug

Little midfield general
Also, 'The new Alan Ball.'
Any player who runs around a lot shouting in a high-pitched voice

Brains of the team
*Player who can punt upfield without hitting the stand roof
and has an O Level in something other than Metalwork*

Coffee-coloured maestro
Same as above, only black

Enigma
Player who wears his shirt outside his shorts

Needs to improve work rate
Needs to tuck his shirt inside his shorts

Too easily knocked off the ball
Has heart the size of a Brussels sprout

That tackle was a little over the top
That tackle was a lobotomy job

Vulnerable at the back
My granny could have put six past them today

Respected throughout the game
Description of centre-half even his mother's terrified of

Distinguished
*Description of any ex-player who's managed to avoid bankruptcy proceedings,
divorce, or arrest for vagrancy since he retired from game*

Professional
Doesn't have sex the night before a game

Dedicated
Doesn't have sex during the season at all

Creative
Shags like a rabbit

Versatile
Pretty awful wherever you play him

Courageous
Falls over in the penalty area a lot, has dents in his forehead left by opponents' boots, spends a lot of time at the dentist and has a nose which goes in three different directions

Uncompromising
Pockmarked face, kicks anything that moves

Emergent football nation
Team full of lookalike midgets of Arab extraction, usually coached by English manager sacked by League club for gross immorality

Playboy image
Its owner drinks Bacardi and Coke, wears a cream mohair suit and screws all the directors' wives

Groin strain
Injury suffered by owner of playboy image

The player they're all talking about
I've just read a piece about him in today's paper

I expect he's wondering what he has to do to score
I hope the viewers can't lipread because he's just quoted Kenneth Tynan

Not, perhaps, the player he was in '82
Looks like the drying-out clinic didn't solve anything

And there's _____, at 40 still very much a vital part of his team
Good heavens, I thought he was dead

(In game against England) And sadly Getemov is gushing blood from a six-inch deep wound in his forehead and looks as though he will take no further part in this match
Thank God for that, the Russians have lost their best player

He's scored! He's scored!
I'm afraid I can't tell you who's scored, but it wasn't a woman

That's it! 2–0
I'm afraid I can't tell you who got that one either, but I can count to two

And the ball went over the line and into the back of the net
If I keep this up long enough, maybe the producer will tell me who's scored

Some of this material originally appeared in the *Sunday Express* magazine and is reproduced with their kind permission

WHERE ARE THEY NOW?
AN A-Z OF WORLD CUP HISTORY

TIM WHITBY

Nelson is remembered for kissing Hardy, King Alfred for burning the cakes and Gordon Banks for saving Pele's header at the far post in Mexico in 1970. Such is fame. World Cup history is a catalogue of memorable moments: the great cock-ups and the great successes. But what happens after the event to the players, managers and referees who have achieved Warhol's 'fifteen minutes of fame'?

Algerians

Lakhdar Belloumi (do you know any others?) will forever be remembered for making one and scoring the winner against the West Germans in Spain. African footballer of the year 1985, transferred from Mascara to NPO in Oran last year. Has been suffering from an ankle injury but should be back in time.

Banks, Gordon

Famous for that Pele save in 1970 (who cares that we lost the game). Now runs Gordon Banks Sales and Promotion, Sileby, Leicestershire, entertaining clients on behalf of their companies. 'We will organise a day out at the races, a snooker evening . . . we take the work off their hands.' Helps coach Villa keepers once a week.

Battiston

See Schumacher

Brazil

Team of the seventies – 'natural footballers', i.e. clearly brought up kicking pawpaws on a beach and therefore had an unfair advantage over the developed nations. What are they doing now that they are too old to play soccer?:

Carlos Alberto
Successfully managed Flamengo and Corinthians, and disappointed not to be running the national side.

Gerson
Respected sports commentator. He is likely to be in Mexico this year as 'team supervisor'.

Jairzinho
Still playing in Ecuador.

Pele
Pepsi-Cola PR consultant. Film star and soon to be US TV actor. At one time it was thought he would run for President but he clearly feels it best to get some screen experience first.

Rivelino
Veteran player, also in the 'used car' business with his uncle.

Socrates
Still plays for Flamengo, still smokes 60 a day, still plays the guitar, still writes poetry, in short, still behaves like a typical Brazilian player.

Tostao
The man who suffered a detached retina has now finished his studies and is an eye surgeon in Brazil.

Bonetti, Peter
Chelsea and England keeper. Brilliant for Chelsea, but will always be remembered as the man who let in the Gerd Muller goal in 1970 which put England out of the cup. Now coaches Chelsea's goalkeepers.

Bremner, Billy
Most aggressive Scottish midfield player until Souness. He now manages Leeds United; and does the odd bit of gardening – 'it's not the be all and end all, but then neither is football.'

Charlton, Jack
Giraffe-like defender and now a fully-fledged polymathic man. A manager, a television pundit, a huntsman, and now the first Englishman to manage the Eire national side.

Conti, Bruno
Very handsome Italian left-winger, broke defenders' spirits and women's hearts in Spain. Brilliant dribbler, even if he does hog it. Still playing for Roma and may be in Mexico.

Coppell, Steve
Sadly retired from international football after his knee injuries. Became the youngest manager in the League when he joined Crystal Palace. 'It's a long way second best to playing, but still better than work.'

Cruyff, Johan
The Dutch Master. Evasive on and off the pitch. (Presently being investigated for non-payment of tax in Spain.) Currently the coach for Ajax – official title 'technical manager' since he doesn't have a coaching certificate.

Duff ideas

ENGLAND
Bulldog Bobby (England's ghastly mascot in Spain)
Petrol Station World Cup Medals (1970)
All unlamented and, to our great relief, unreplaced.

NORTHERN IRELAND
Yer Man (thuggish little mascot sporting a cap and scarf, Spain '82)
Won't be making an appearance in Mexico, and won't be replaced.

SCOTLAND

Sandy (the 'cute' cartoon for Spain)

Roary, Superscot the Lion (for Argentina)

R.I.P. but the SFA are persevering with a cartoon lion, wittily named McMex.

England managers (Alf, Don, Joe, Ron and Walter)

Ramsey, Sir Alf

England's most famous manager. 'Went on' to manage Birmingham (briefly) and coach in Greece. Now completely retired from football; watches Ipswich fixtures.

Revie, Don

The Stalin of English football. Much loved while in power, now the subject of revisionist historians. After he 'left' England he went to Dubai: 'We were there for six years and had a lovely time.' Now living in Ascot and works as a director of Total Sports, a Windsor-based company who provide the hospitality for sporting events.

Mercer, Joe

Completely retired. 'The nearest I come to football is the weekly spot-the-ball competition.' Living in The Wirral.

Having a lovely time – Don Revie of England and Dubai

Ron Greenwood in the England days, flashing a well-turned ankle

Greenwood, Ron

Enjoying retirement near Bournemouth. Ron's forays into the world of football are restricted to the occasional Radio 2 commentary round-up.

Winterbottom, Sir Walter

Survived four World Cup campaigns, now honorary vice-president of the FA. 'I'm now busy trying to keep myself fit playing bowls and golf.'

Footballs

Where are the leather puddings of yesteryear? Replaced by oversized ping-pong balls called España and Azteca. (Clearly another example of bias against the Northern European game.)

Eusebio

The great hero of Portuguese football and the top scorer (9) in the '66 finals. Still called the Black Panther – 'even when I'm walking in the street' – now assistant coach (to John Mortimer) at Benfica. 'I like football; it's my life.'

One of the best memories of '66 – Portugal's hero Eusebio

Gentile

Great Italian defender. Some players are famous for what they did; Gentile was famous for who he did – Maradona, Zico, the rest of the Brazilian forward line and the West German midfield. Still playing for Fiorentina but not likely to grace Mexico.

Jimmy Greaves, in the days before he wore all those flash jerseys

Willie Johnston demonstrating his on-field speed ...

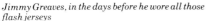

Greaves, Jimmy	The best English forward never to play in the 1966 World Cup Final. Maintains connection with football as an academic authority on Scottish goalkeepers but his primary commitment is to the world of Light Entertainment.
Hector, Kevin	The man who almost was. Remember England v Poland '73? England need to win to qualify for Munich. Hector, Sir Alf's 87th-minute sub, hits the crossbar with seconds to go and England go out. Currently managing the Stuff of Life pub in Ticknall, Derbyshire. 'He's doing a marvellous job pulling in the crowds,' says the landlady.
Hurst, Geoff	Hat-trick hero of 1966. After a spell with England on the coaching team, now a director of Motor-Plan in Dagenham, specialists in mechanical breakdown insurance. 'I'm trying to retire gracefully from football.'
Johnstone, Jimmy	Original Scottish wizard of the dribble, famous for his speed on the turn. Now a van driver for Lafferty the builders in Glasgow, and coaching Celtic youth part-time: 'Working with the boys keeps your eye in – I train them twice a week, Tuesday and Thursday evenings.'
Johnston, Willie	Another Scottish winger famous for his 'speed': took reactivin tablets in the 1978 World Cup. Was banned from ever playing for Scotland again and flown home in disgrace. Owns the Port Brae Bar in Kirkcaldy, and plays the odd charity match.

Jules Rimet Trophy   Awarded outright to Brazil after their third victory, the Trophy was stolen from Brazilian FA headquarters in Rio de Janeiro in August 1980 and melted down. Kodak presented the Brazilians with an exact replica in June 1981. This is now in the bank and a copy of the replica is back on display in Rio.

Lee, Francis   The great football success story. Earned penalties for England, earned multi-millions by the age of 40. Given up football altogether, now trains racehorses, runs a stud farm and owns a paper factory. 'I go running occasionally but that's all.'

MacLeod, Ally   The man who inspired a nation but not a team. Elaborate and expensive preparation (air-freighted haggis) couldn't save Scotland from humiliation and finally disgrace in 1978. Now back managing Ayr United – crowds of a few thousand in the Scottish First Division – his first club, his third spell in charge. Owns a coffee shop and a pub, Ally's, in Ayr and the Tudor Bar in Kilmarnock. 'I might arrive in the big time again. I'm not too old yet.'

Marsh, Rodney   One of the great entertainers. Along with Best and Di Stefano, he never played in the World Cup finals. Coaching Tampa Bay Rowdies in America.

Masson, Don   Scotland's '78 game against Peru in Argentina. A win would have assured a place in the quarter-finals and at 1–1 Masson

A Mona Lisa smile from Ally MacLeod, mastermind of Scotland's ill-fated '78 attempt

The legend of Loftus Road – Rodney Marsh, now a Rowdy

took a penalty. Queroga (El Loco) saved and Peru went on to win 3–1. Scotland were out. After only three months at Kettering Town, abandoned non-League football for the sun. Now coaches in the US and Down Under but lives in Burton Joyce, just outside Nottingham, and is involved with small building company, purchasing property.

Moore, Bobby
Captain of England's victorious 1966 team, will also be remembered as the man accused of stealing a bracelet in Bogota (1970). Now manages Southend.

Paine, Terry
Much-capped Southampton and England winger who missed out on the '66 final. Now coaching in South Africa, through his own company Terry Paine Sports. PO Box 1088, Bedford View, 2008 South Africa.

Peters, Martin
The 'ghost'. After a less than successful foray into football management, now works alongside Geoff Hurst. Plays in the Dennis Waterman Charity XI, which is sponsored by Motor-Plan. 'I'm still a mug for a game of football.'

Pickles
The dog who sniffed out the Jules Rimet Trophy from under a bush after it was stolen in 1966. Several years later hung himself on his lead chasing after a cat: a sorry end for a dog who did so much for world football. Now at peace in his owner's garden in Lingfield, Surrey: 'I won't part with him. He's done me too many favours.'

The late, great Pickles, the dog who saved the 1966 World Cup

Peru keeper Quiroga tells his defence to take it easy – after all, it is Argentina they're playing

Quiroga (El Loco)   Crazy Peruvian keeper. Superb tackler on the halfway line. He will be forever remembered as the man who saved Don Masson's penalty in Argentina, putting Scotland out of the Cup. Sadly Peru haven't qualified this year so he'll be staying in Lima.

Referees

Taylor, Jack
One of the greatest English referees. Controlled the '74 Holland v West Germany final, when he gave a penalty against the Germans before they had even touched the ball. Now back up north running his building firm full time.

Thomas, Clive
One of the greatest Welsh referees. Famous for blowing 'full time' between the moment the ball left a Brazilian head and the moment it hit the back of the Swedish net. He did not go on to referee the '74 final between Holland and West Germany. 'I'm not a bitter man. I've got a very good job with Office Cleaning Services.'

Schumacher, Harald   Still Germany's number one goalkeeper despite knocking out Battiston's teeth in the France v West Germany semi-final in Spain, and so keeping his side in the competition.

Stiles, Nobby   The most extraordinary football hero of modern times, remembered for his jig around Wembley in 1966, holding aloft the Jules Rimet trophy, and sporting his toothless grin.

Is Nobby Stiles demonstrating how he lost those teeth? Martin Peters looks on in the '66 World Cup Final

Now in charge of the youth team at W.B.A. 'I play the odd game of golf when I get the chance and the odd charity match, only the odd one because I'm getting old – the legs get old.'

Tarantini

Argentinian star full-back in '78. Came to England after Villa and Ardiles and signed for Birmingham but wisely flew home. He now plays in the Argentinian First Division.

Tomaszewski, Jan

Polish goalie who frustrated England at Wembley in 1973. Famously labelled 'a clown' by Brian Clough. Now assistant manager at LQS and training keepers at small clubs around Lodz in Poland.

Villa, Ricky

The handsomest of the three Argentinians to come to England. (The Good, The Bad and Ardiles.) After leaving Spurs he played in the US but has since moved to Colombia where he plays for Cali.

West Germany

Paul Breitner in pre-Mao days

England's greatest rivals. England have never minded being defeated by out-and-out foreigners. They have unfair advantages: they can play at altitude, in extreme heat, on pot-holed, pampas-like pitches and are natural ball-players ('silky skills'). Being defeated, however, by Northern Europeans who go pink and sweat in the heat, just like us, has always been galling. What has happened to England's least favourite Germans:

Beckenbauer, Franz
Now managing the national team.

Breitner, Paul
Last heard of converting the citizens of Munich to Mao.

Hoeness, Uli
Now managing Bayern Munich.

Maier, Sepp
Managing a tennis centre in Munich.

Muller, Gerd
Now managing restaurants in Florida, US.

Netzer, Gunter
In his last season as Hamburg's manager.

Wilson, Ray

England 1966 full-back, now has 'no connections at all with the game.' Owns a small farm at the foot of the Pennines. Better known as a funeral director.

Zoff, Dino

The great Italian goalkeeper. The oldest player to represent his country in the World Cup. At 40 he captained his side to victory in Spain. Now assistant to Bearzot, manager of the national side.

FROM ALLY'S ARMY TO BOBBY'S B-SIDE

RICK SHEARMAN

The World Cup isn't only about football – it also involves merchandising, particularly of nasty records. Rick Shearman of The Sunday Times *has agreed to become our music critic and now analyses some recent (and not-so-recent) offerings.*

Teenyboppers everywhere got a very nasty shock indeed on a balmy Thursday evening in May 1970. I know I did.

Tuning into *Top of the Pops* hoping to catch a glimpse of Marvin Gaye, or the erstwhile future of rock'n'roll Norman Greenbaum singing 'Spirit in the Sky', millions instead saw that the number one position had been occupied by a bunch of footballers. Beaming away, singing (for want of a better word) something about how much the people of Britain were going to miss them, and sounding in urgent need of altitude training where the high notes were concerned (an omen, as it turned out). The song was, of course, 'Back Home'.

That was the first World Cup single, and when England failed to qualify in '74 and '78 the thought that without a World Cup squad there could be no World Cup single was a source of considerable consolation for the discerning listener.

'Back Home' was also the first proper football single, in the strict sense of all the lads getting together to commit to vinyl their excitement at getting to Wembley/Division One/score or whatever. Sixteen years on, the football single is a genre in its own right, and one that has had its moments. Usually, though, no more than one or two per season.

World Cup years, however, are something else. For a start there are the spin-offs: not only do we get the players themselves making their bid for pop immortality, but we find dozens of others hoping to cash in on World Cup fever. Many of them on respectable record labels, and featuring old favourites usually only heard at Christmas, like choirs of cutey-pie kiddies, or dogs trying to be Bulldog Bobby.

The second special thing about World Cup singles is what they might tell us about the teams themselves. Compare, for example, 'Ossie's Dream' – happy, confident, uninhibited – with 'This Time' – the England team sounding like zombies. One team won in style, the other went out in silence after two mind-numbing goalless draws. Coincidence?

You can take this further. Look at England's choice of song, of songwriter, of production, of image projected; from 'Back Home' to 'This Time'/'Fly the Flag' all have been about as enterprising as Don Revie. Fear of failure seems to dog England's records like it dogs their performances, and when a line like 'We are Ron's 22' can be delivered without the slightest suggestion of irony you get a feeling that maybe the on-field paralysis that grips so many England sides might not be unconnected with the conservatism that seems to run right through the England set-up.

Look then at Scotland. Their singles feature wit and invention in abundance, but more than that they exude a feeling that Scottish style, Scottish self-belief can, will, pull them through anything. Knowing that they might not be the greatest but that if they *aim* to play football as it should be played they'll at least go down in style. If you remember Scotland v Holland in 1978, with a soundtrack of the immortal words from 'Ally's Tartan Army' – 'We're representing Britain and we've got to do or die/Cos England cannae do it cos they didnae qualify' – you get the picture.

The point is, of course, that if a team can't show any imagination when they're larking about in a recording studio, it doesn't exactly bode well for their forthcoming on-field exploits either. Know what I mean?

Anyway, the singles themselves. Most, admittedly, sound like tunes considered too dull for the Eurovision Song Contest with the lyrics hastily rearranged. On the other hand, there are a number of football classics – sonatas for centre-forwards. And I'll take a good deal of convincing that this one doesn't fit squarely into the second category:

ENGLAND SQUAD 1970
'Back Home'

It started here.

ANDY CAMERON
'Ally's Tartan Army'

Not only a candidate for the greatest football song of all time, but also one of those rare all-purpose insert-your-own words tunes, the song seems to sum up everything about Scotland '78. Was Ally's army the team, the fans, or both? Full of optimism, daring and unforgettably daft lines like 'He's our Muhammad Ally, he's Alastair MacLeod'. Genius.

ROD STEWART
'Ole Ola'
('We're gonna bring that World Cup back from over thar')

Another from '78, setting Mr Cameron's sentiments to a jaunty Latin beat. Again an abundance of wit, but the B side – Rod with the Scottish squad singing 'Que Sera' and 'I'd walk a million miles for one of your goals' – should be played only to get rid of unwanted guests.

SCOTLAND SQUAD 1974
'Easy, Easy'

A Top 20 smasheroo, and an amazing contemporary document – football meets real pop for the first time. The thumping beat could well be the Glitter Band, and so could the vocals were it not for the highbrow content like 'Yaba daba doo, we support the boys in blue'. The title is pushing even Scottish self-confidence a bit far though; 'Difficult, Difficult' might have been a more honest assessment.

GENE FITZPATRICK
'Viva Ireland'

A rarity from '82, this same tune also appeared as 'Viva England' (courtesy of Ian 'Sludge' Lees) and 'Viva Scotland' (Ben Gunn). But Fitzpatrick, a nightclub crooner with an emerald satin shirt, a sizeable waistline and grin like one of Norman Whiteside's tackles, gets the vote.

SCOTLAND 1982 FEATURING GORDON JOHN SINCLAIR
'If Dreams Come True'

More Scottish genius, possibly the only high spot in the career of B. A. Robertson, but loses marks for a rather unpleasant twist in the tail.

SERIOUS DRINKING:
'Bobby Moore Is Innocent'

Made in about 1983, a Norwich band asks the one Mexico question that really matters. Never mind Bonetti's lapse – what happened to the jewellery?

DANA WITH THE 1982 NORTHERN IRELAND SQUAD
'Yer Man'

A massive credibility boost for Dana, otherwise flip it over for a classically awful tear-jerking monologue featuring lines like 'It's Bingy . . . he's yer man' while the Londonderry Air plays softly in the background.

ENGLAND 1982
'This Time'

'To win them all . . . is what we'll set out to do' – clearly Don Howe didn't help with the lyrics. Believed to be the worst football single of all time, until:

ENGLAND 1982
'Fly the Flag'

The B side, showing a bit too much heavy nationalism for many people's liking. Believed not to have been a hit in Buenos Aires.

And so to 1986. There are no certainties in football, as they say, and this could be the most open World Cup in years. But whatever the on-field outcome, you can bet your bottom dollar on one thing. There will be some very dodgy sounds indeed coming out of your radio this May and June. You have been warned.

THE INNER GAME

One of the old chestnuts of soccer is the saying that a footballer's brains are all in his boots. But what goes on inside his head is pretty important as well. Need convincing? Just read on and see what the professionals have to say about the footballing psyche.

The winning goal in the World Cup could be scored by a Rescued, having been set up by an Ignorer after a Squasher has done all the hard work. That is according to a theory of behaviour – the S.I.R. system – developed by psychologist and broadcaster Dr Tony Lake.

S.I.R. was designed as a means of counselling in work and employment, but it is so effective as a model that it adapts readily to football. It is based on a theory of personality types which are variations in a basic system of personality.

To explain: since Freud, psychologists have increasingly regarded personality as *structured,* i.e. a system rather than a random collection of traits. Our individual differences can be explained as variations of the same basic system, and in terms of a limited number of common variations or 'personality types'.

S.I.R. is one method of identifying such types and explaining the influences which make a person one type rather than another.

THE THEORY

As babies, our behaviour tends to be reflex. Then, during childhood, we learn gradually to control our actions so we can take our place in the adult world. The behavioural patterns which result make up our self-control system. As adults, it is during crisis points in our lives that this control system is brought into play.

Parenting is a crucial factor in learning self-control. In childhood and adolescence, they teach us how to react in crises – situations that demand a reaction so innate and unselfconscious that we are unable to deal with it with our usual deliberate, appropriate or ideal behaviour.

A child sees the way his parents react to their crises. Vitally, he observes their unpremeditated response to his own 'bad' actions – perhaps they show fear or anger or embarrassment or anxiety – as well as learning self-control through their discipline and nurturing.

S.I.R. is based on three main types of parental control.

S = SQUASH

The parent, in order to express fear and anger, and control the child, uses violence (mild or severe) or the threat of violence. Abuse can be verbal (grumbling or sarcasm, for instance) rather than physical. In its most distressing manifestation, it will result in the 'battered baby' syndrome.

In adult life, a child who has had Squash control will manifest as a Squasher (the active, extrovert version) or a Squashed (passive and introvert). In crisis, Squashers defend themselves by hitting out first and denigrating other people. A squashed will take the rap and apologise cravenly.

I = IGNORE

Here, parental control depends on rejecting the child or banishing it (to its bedroom, for instance). In its most severe form, this will result in a child being neglected and starved to death. As an adult, he will become an Ignorer (ignores problems and denies anything's wrong, refuses help) or an Ignored (feels ashamed and guilty, hides or runs away, suppresses feelings).

R = RESCUE

In this instance, parents deal with problems either by getting the child to 'rescue' them ('Don't do that, it'll give me a headache') or rescuing the child before he makes a mistake, thus stunting his ability to learn from it. The adult Rescuer puts others before himself in a crisis, while the Rescued waits for someone else to get him off the hook.

© Tony Lake 1986

Squashers like to get their shot in first. Their ruling verb is 'do'. The ultimate competitors of this world, they can't tolerate failure and daren't lose. They go mad at the prospect of being beaten at tiddlywinks, confuse bellowing their heads off with civilised debate and practise their golf swings while sitting on the toilet. Squashers aren't necessarily physically violent. The really successful ones have developed better methods of keeping everyone in line than courting arrest for actual bodily harm (though when squashers need to they aren't shy of relying on sheer lung-power – a squasher organising his midfield at Stamford Bridge has sometimes been audible at Old Trafford). But top squashers are adept at 'eye-zapping', or quelling dissidents with a look.

Some also stop the natives from getting restless by making a career of Ill Health. When sick, they carry on nobly, while making sure everyone knows about their housemaid's knee/back trouble/ impacted wisdom teeth (squashers *never* have nervous breakdowns).

They are the leaders of the pack, and sometimes its bullies and boors as well. They tend to clone in a crisis, kicking out the showy Ignorers and namby-pamby Rescuers and getting in more of their own kind. (Think of the football manager who drops half of his regular team for not trying and drafts in the keen young newcomers from the reserves.)

Their inspiration is *energy*. They've always got that much more of it than anyone else (Margaret Thatcher is the Squasher par excellence), so they run committees, other people's lives and the London Marathon, often all at once. They are motivated by *action* and the pure, undiluted Squasher wouldn't know an abstract concept if it jumped up and waved its knickers in his face.

They feel compelled to do things in the outside world – achieving and attaining. They must be where the action is, otherwise they feel threatened. Naturally, many of them gravitate towards competitive sports where they can get their highs from kicking each other in the groin or bawling out the umpire.

Footballing squashers will sweat blood at training, which is why they often suffer from troublesome long-term injuries – even against their own team-mates they have to compete, and they keep going long after they should have stopped because they can't bear the thought of conceding their place in the side to anyone else.

When they get old, squashers get very irascible and buy large dogs so they can still bark orders at something. They either die in their sleep at a great age thanks to their natural fitness, or keel over with a heart attack trying to beat their sons at tennis.

The **Squashed** are the introvert version of the squashers, and many people alternate between the two sorts of behaviour. While squashers *do,* the squashed are *done by* (or they do it to themselves). The most extreme squashed types apologise to people who tread on their feet, lie back and think of England, and buy faulty double-glazing from door to door salesmen because they can't bring themselves to say No. You can always tell someone who's really severely squashed because their favourite word is 'Sorry'.

Being squashed isn't necessarily synonymous with failure or spine-lessness. The majority of people with this type of personality fit very comfortably into the scheme of things, maybe never winning the big jackpots of life, but never sitting down on the seat where the paint hasn't quite dried either. Squashed types who do become famous figures can be very complex or tortured personalities, like John McEnroe. 'There's someone who was very squashed as a child,' comments Tony Lake. 'If you listen to his outbursts, you can hear him squashing himself.'

A mildly squashed personality will make a very good second-in-command.

In football, he'll be happy to be the captain's sidekick, not embarrass or antagonise him by competing for the leadership. He'll back up his captain on the pitch by getting the others to follow through his orders, will assist in goals and provide service for the target men rather than seeking to cover himself in glory. In order to mitigate the worst effects of the squasher, he'll often act as his mouthpiece, substituting the diplomatic, 'The boss says . . .' for 'Do this' or 'Do that'. Like squashers, the squashed are compulsive trainers, mainly because they like doing things to themselves.

Of the three players in midfield, you'll usually find that two of them have to exhibit mild squashed characteristics in order not to clash with the chief motivator.

SQUASH types in football

There are likely to be several squashers in a team – including the captain. But he won't be one of the really aggressive, threatening ones. He's far more likely to be the mild, flexible type of squasher who can wield the necessary discipline without alienating his team. He's a master of the eye-zap and the quiet but unignorable reprimand.

Another sort of football squasher is the big, clogging, lovable centre-half, the sort who fractures an opponent's leg but sends flowers to the hospital.

Famous football squashers: Kenny Dalglish ('He's assertive and confident,' says Tony Lake, 'but with a controlled personality which enables him to control others') and Bryan Robson ('A mild squasher, flexible, steady, not easily discouraged and commands respect for his deeds'). Most managers have a strong element of the squasher in them – think of Billy Bremner, Jack Charlton, Lawrie McMenemy, Brian Clough – because otherwise they would never be able to synthesise the team.

Ray Wilkins is a good example of mild squashed, says Tony Lake. 'He can be a squasher at times but basically he feels happier as second-in-command. He's probably the type of oldest son in a family whose every scrap of talent has been moulded and made the most of by a caring but authoritative parent. He could be a delegated child – doing for Daddy what Daddy couldn't do.'

It's often Squashed types who get the jobs as assistant managers, then, when the manager gets the sack, have to take over. Then they need either to develop the Squasher mechanism in their personalities, or fail because they can't function without a squasher to lead them.

Ignorers will do anything to get noticed, from wearing a revolving bow-tie and a sombrero that lights up to abseiling up the side of the Houses of Parliament. Their refusal to eat up their greens as children was punished by two hours' solitary in the bedroom, which has resulted in an adult determination never to be anywhere but the centre of attention, and a lifelong horror of cabbage.

Ignore types are motivated by acquiring and receiving – their ruling verb is 'have'. They want applause, acclaim, space, wardrobes full of clothes, a big house and, naturally, money. They like lots of room in which to manoeuvre, either physical space (territory) or an uncluttered head. But if they're denied that space they don't moan like their Squash counterparts; they simply take what little they have – a bedsit the size of a postage stamp, a desk in a typing pool, a tiny piece of paper – and turn it into something exquisite. Footballers who can do magic things in the six-yard box, who can take the ball on their shoulder, let it bounce to the knee, shift onto the other foot, turn and sell the keeper a dummy and all inside the circumference of a beer mat, probably spent a lot of time being sent to the broom cupboard when they were kids.

Ignored people are the passive, introvert counterparts of the Ignorers. The worst ones react to being treated as *persona non grata* by their parents by spending the rest of their lives only semi-aware that they exist. In relationships, they turn the other person – friend, spouse, colleague, boss – into the parent who ignores them. They are the women who buy all those grey crimplene trouser suits and brown plastic shoes from mail order (I bet you always wondered who it was) and the men who fill up the non-smokers compartments of the 7.10 to Victoria on weekdays. Their favourite design pattern is camouflage.

Ignored types sometimes become actors or newsreaders but then make a career out of coming on in the second act and saying, 'Mr Pettifer is waiting to see you, my lord,' or doing the late night wrap-up on Radio Orkney. The quintessential Ignored motto is Think Librarian. Even if an Ignored makes it to the National Theatre and the title role in *Hamlet*, he sounds like Hamlet played by a librarian.

Like Ignorers, they're motivated by *having*, but in their case it's often skills for which they can gain recognition and acceptance. They're particularly proud of their own cleverness and often cherish a better opinion of themselves than the world at large – at the same time doing nothing to raise the opinion of that world. Sometimes they have secrets, and fantasies about themselves which they don't share, like Walter Mitty. Of all the groups, they're the least generous. A real Ignored is so mean that if he had whisky on his breath he wouldn't let you smell it.

IGNORE types in football

The Ignored is the show-off and the charming, comical clown. Malcolm Allison is the typical example of this personality. Here are many of the showmen and characters of football: Stan Bowles, Charlie George, Rodney Marsh, Steve Archibald, George Best, Charlie Nicholas. Terry Venables, though he has a strong Squasher side, also has a bit of the Ignorer in his personality – remember how he found fame on TV by wiggling his eyebrows?

'They're usually very clever people with great skill,' says Tony Lake. 'They like dressing up, often in flamboyant clothes, or they have gimmicks like Big Mal's hat and cigar.'

When an Ignorer scores a goal, his typical reaction is not to punch the air and rush up for a quick snog with his team-mates, but to stand there or kneel and let the applause wash over him (remember how Peie used to do it?). Ignore types also believe in having lots of hair – 'Some of them like to hide their faces behind a beard,' says Tony Lake. 'Jimmy Hill is a very good example.'

Ignore people, with their special feeling for space, often turn up footballers like Martin Peters (who the opposition ignored at their peril), and Glenn Hoddle, who switches from Ignorer to Ignored and back during many a game.

Highly ignored types don't usually make the team (with one notable exception, as we'll see below). They're more likely to be the administrators, the back-up team, the people in the ticket office. They're very clever at doing things no one else wants to do so they become indispensable.

The notable exception? As Tony Lake points out, 'The goalkeeper is a typical Mild Ignored. It's the job which nobody else wants, he's got his territory marked out by the goalposts and he sets up home in there with his cap and gloves. Although a goalie also has a bit of the squasher in him. That comes out when he organises his defence, tells them what to do and yells at them when they get it wrong.'

On field, an Ignore type can sometimes switch from active to passive and when that happens he'll have a very bad game – he doesn't get the ball passed to him, he drifts out of the action and eventually gets himself dropped from the team. A good example is the prima donna with Ignorer skills who gets a big money transfer and then switches into Ignored mode with the result that the transfer doesn't work out.

Interestingly, three recent England managers seem to have had strong Ignored tendencies – Don Revie, who banished himself to Saudi Arabia, Sir Alf Ramsey who banished himself from football altogether, and Ron Greenwood whose deep-thinking, almost mystic attitude towards football is typical Ignored intellectual style.

Rescuers' parents used manipulation to control them and these poor types have been a soft touch ever since for the assorted inadequates, neurotics and out-and-out loonies who gravitate towards them like pins to a magnet. The rescuer was never allowed to be little himself because in the relationship with his parent there was room for only one child and that was Mummy or Daddy. If when young you were kept in order by being told, 'Don't do that, it'll give me a headache/kill your father/wake granny,' you are probably a rescuer; you had to rescue your parents.

Rescuers are often second sons or daughters, the Good Boys and Good Girls of the family. They have to be grateful for what's done for them. At their best, they're wonderful to have around because they're completely unselfish and always put themselves last. At their worst, they're those scrubbed, earnest-looking people who ring on the door when you've just sat down on the loo, then try and flog you the *Watchtower*.

The ruling verb for Rescue types is 'be' or 'feel'. They're motivated by praise and thanks and their big fear is that they'll be thought self-centred, which is why Rescuers always have a worse standard of living than their friends; when they ask for a pay rise all they get is, 'We're very grateful for all the magnificent work you're doing.'

A lot of sales managers in industry have strong Rescuer tendencies – they're everyone's Mum and Dad. In football, it's the rescuer who encourages the others rather than competing with them (squasher) or doing their own thing (ignorer). Often at a club you'll find the rescuer is in charge of the youth team and he's the one who tries to make the newcomer feel at home. He'll make helpful suggestions without embarrassing anyone in the team and is the one who thinks so-and-so should have his chance.

The Rescuer is usually late because he's so busy helping everyone (Shirley Williams is a typical Rescuer) and if you see a footballer pile into the goalmouth just a split second too late to meet the ball then he's probably a Rescuer who's been too busy seeing another player knows what he's got to do.

Rescued types have no idea of time either, but that's because they've always relied on someone else to get them to wherever they want to be. What the hell, they fill in the hiatus with lots of wonderful anecdotes. On the football field they're the ones who provide the final brilliant touch – or hold play up while writhing on the floor in agony till the physio comes along with his magic sponge. A rescued person has had a parent who did everything for him from lacing up his shoes to finishing his Maths homework to save him getting it wrong.

On a mundane level, rescued types tend to function badly unless someone gives them a long list of instructions. But often they're the geniuses of their group, the temperamental but gifted artists, or at the very least talented operators with a great ability to rip off other people's work.

In football, the Rescued player may be the Golden Boy, the lucky one who gets all the breaks in the game (and of course he has the talent to take advantage of them). He's often the baby of the team and the darling of the crowd. He'll get the sort of goals that the other ones half-make because he's got this strange instinct for where to be at the right time. People call them easy goals, but of course they just look that way.

'Players like this have never been discouraged so they've never had crises of confidence,' says Tony Lake. 'On the other hand, they tend to be intuitive players and bad at learning new tricks, so managers shouldn't try and get them to change their style.'

RESCUE types in football

Bobby Robson – 'I see him as the archetypal sales manager,' says Tony Lake. 'Mother and father and wet nurse, the kind who slaps players down when they need it but is too kindly and caring to be an enthusiastic squasher.' Ron Atkinson – 'Obviously there's a lot of the squasher there, but if you listen to him he's got a very reassuring quality about him.' Kerry Dixon, Jimmy Greaves, Denis Law and Bobby Charlton all have Rescued tendencies.

What is the behavioural style of British football?

Anglo-Saxon football is Squasher football – the battering-ram approach, wear 'em down, charge through all the obstacles, keep going non-stop. Scotland and Northern Ireland share some of these tendencies but have distinguishing qualities. With Scotland, a much stronger element of Ignorer showmanship is encouraged. Northern Ireland, with their small, loyal, close-knit squad, seem to have developed the Rescuer tendency of players motivated by supporting each other.

One problem, when it comes to international football, is that brilliance in sport is unEnglish. You can have individual brilliance (though even then it's treated with suspicion) but not team brilliance. Moreover, the concept of a homogeneous team, of the whole being greater than the sum of its parts – which often makes for mediocrity through the crushing of individual flair – is very Squasher.

'This is how League football works in England,' says Tony Lake, 'so internationally England has a problem because international football doesn't work that way. Where you've got a strong League that's proud of its own unique style and culture it makes it more difficult to find players flexible enough to adapt to another style of play.'

Which of our players are best suited psychologically to compete in this World Cup?

According to Tony Lake, Ignorers will probably adapt the best, and Ignored. They will work very hard to win the applause and approval of the crowd by using individual flair. Rescued, with their ability to capitalise on the half chance, will probably retain more energy than the Rescuers, who'll be too worried about everyone else's suffering in the conditions to play effective football. Squashers, unfortunately, will merely increase their work rate to compensate for their lack of brilliance – and fry to a crisp under the Mexico sun.

Why do two teams of opposing styles produce a less entertaining game than two similar ones?

International football de-skills many good club players, because a lot of the predictability of other players disappears. The more separate a national style is, the harder it is to play against opponents without that style. So when two sides of opposing styles are drawn together, one is forced to become like the other. If you get a greyhound versus a bulldog, the bulldog will have to become a greyhound or vice versa. Clearly, the side which is compelled to adapt is already at a disadvantage.

On the other hand, teams of similar styles find it easier to play together and produce a more flowing game because many split-second decisions in a match depend on what a player predicts the other team will do. 'Teams don't just compete, they interact,' says Tony Lake. 'We've been going on about the differences for years but actually it's the common factors that are relevant.'

'OUT OF THE MOUTHS OF . . .' THE BEST OF THE WORLD CUP QUOTES

'Everything I know of my fellow man, I owe to football,' to paraphrase Albert Camus, and people have been making quotable quotes on the same subject ever since. Here's the pick of the star performers' thoughts on Mexico '86 and other World Cup matters.

THE ANIMALS ARE COMING.
Headline in Monterrey newspaper after England draw to play there

Bobby Robson with Monterrey's local paper showing reaction to the prospect of an invasion of England fans

If you want a nice time and some enjoyable matches it's a good draw. If you want to make progress it's a nasty little group. But it's not as bad as Scotland's.
Martin O'Neill, Northern Ireland

Now all we need is a team.
Brazilian journalist after Brazil qualify for finals

It's going to be a draw between your teams, we know that. And for us, four years of hard work will just vanish.
Mircea Lucescu, team manager of Romania, before the England v Northern Ireland qualifying match that put Romania out of the World Cup

Romanian manager Mircea Lucescu caught in mid-quote

People have told me that I will have problems because I used to play alongside some of my national team stars. But I don't think that friendship is incompatible with professional respect.
Henri Michel, on becoming manager of France

Henri Michel – still friendly

After we beat Belgium to reach the European semi-finals the players were celebrating until three the next morning. Yes, and drinking and smoking. If the players drink a beer, or 10 or 15 beers I don't mind... as long as they are all together at lunch the next day. What matters to me is that they can go out onto the pitch when it is time and do their job to the best of their ability.
Sepp Piontek, manager of Denmark

I want an end to all this frustrating pushing the ball backwards and forwards by fat-cat professionals – men with 400,000DM (£107,000) contracts, Cartier gold chains around their necks, sunglasses in their tailored silk shirt pockets and Porsches in the stadium car parks.
Franz Beckenbauer on his arrival as manager of West Germany

When European teams try to play the South American way they usually end up by getting mixed up and frustrated, because natural talent cannot be transmitted by orders of the coach.
Argentina manager Carlos Bilardi

I was responsible for Eder giving up smoking.
Tele Santana, ex-manager of Brazil, on his contribution to the game

A footballer is someone who can make his feet obey his head.
Tibor Nyilisi, captain of Hungary

When a fetish is worn by a player or placed near the goals in the hope that this can change the course of the game, this superstitious belief can cause reactions in the stadium, even leading to serious incidents.
Ethiopian journalist Yidnekatchew Tessema on the problems of African football

We will win the World Cup.
Alf Ramsey, manager of England, in 1964

The mask of a defeated man – Alf Ramsey after England's defeat by Poland in '73

177

Who's Kissing Me Now?
Title of book by West German World Cup-winning goalie Sepp Maier, which claimed to lift the lid off the antics of Beckenbauer, Rummenigge, Hoeness, Breitner et al

Everything was perfect.
Franz Beckenbauer after West Germany had beaten Czechoslovakia 5–1 in WC Qualifying Group 6

Every team playing a European style will struggle because of the oxygen debt caused by heat and humidity.
Northern Ireland manager Billy Bingham on the problems of playing in Mexico

I told the players that anything we could do this year would work to our advantage in the World Cup. Courtesy costs nothing. They should kiss babies, sign autographs, pose for photographs and give interviews.
Bobby Robson on how to improve England's image abroad after the tragedy of Brussels

I think it is easier to savour the pleasure of victory or to share the grief of defeat together. Those hours are helping to make the team feel a unit and not a bunch of strangers recruited for one match only.
Franz Beckenbauer on why he makes his players stay on for a day after an international game.

The hell of Mexico.
Polish newspaper's description of Monterrey

If it were possible, I would play until I was 100. I have seen too many players who have left the game and just live on their memories
Diego Maradona

We know the West Germans. We see them every week on television. They play machine football.
Sepp Piontek, manager of Denmark, on his first-round opponents

I know absolutely nothing about them.
Cayetano Re, manager of Paraguay, on his group opponents Iraq

I've never believed in staying around somewhere when I'm not wanted.
Republic of Ireland manager Eoin Hand, announcing his intention to step down after failing to get his side to Mexico

Not wanted on voyage: Republic of Ireland manager Eoin Hand

Bans will be strictly enforced on smoking, alcohol, large flags and standing up (except after Danish goals).
Warning to Danish fans before Russia v Denmark in Moscow. Russia won the Group 6 match 1–0

It's great, just great,
absolutely great.
*Tony Waiters, Canada manager,
commenting on their draw against
France, Russia and Hungary*

*Tony Waiters, obviously enjoying life as manager of
Canada*

Fortunately we're meeting them at
football, not ice hockey.
*French goalie Joel Bats on learning
of the draw with Canada, the Soviet
Union and Hungary*

At least this will ensure we don't go
to Mexico overburdened with
optimism.
*Scottish manager Alex Ferguson on
Scotland's group, made up of West
Germany, Denmark and Uruguay*

Kenny is not just an individual.
What makes him great is that he
brings other players into the game.
Bob Paisley on Kenny Dalglish

You must be joking.
*Sir Alf Ramsey at a press conference
in Mexico City after the affair of
Bobby Moore's stolen bracelet,
replying to local journalist who
welcomed him to Mexico*

The whole team, if possible.
*Czechoslovakia manager Masopust,
when asked who he would drop for
the forthcoming game against West
Germany after drawing 0–0 with
Malta in WC Qualifying Group 2*

I don't like playing against English
teams. They don't give you any
room in the penalty area and they
never lose concentration in defence.
They are very strong physically and
they fight for every ball.
Tibor Nyilasi, captain of Hungary

I am a very proud man.
*Wales manager Mike England after
the 1–0 victory over Scotland in WC
Qualifying Group 7 at Hampden*

What a load of rubbish.
Scotland supporters after same

This is the worst thing that has
happened in my seven years as
manager.
*Alf Ramsey after moves to bring a
charge of theft against Bobby Moore
in Bogota in 1970*

This has been my worst 6 days
in 35 years in football.
*Bobby Robson, leaving for the
England tour of Mexico '85 in the
wake of the Brussels disaster*

England have had problems with
the national team simply because
they have so many players to choose
from.
Mircea Lucescu

Bobby Robson's natural expression
is that of a man who fears he might
have left the gas on.
David Lacey

My wife tells me the game has changed me; that I've become more of a mean guy than I used to be.
Bobby Robson

For a continental coach, a team is a bit like a patchwork quilt – they want to stitch onto their elegant play the commitment of the British player.
Irving Scholar, chairman of Tottenham Hotspur

We are up to the neck in great players and we couldn't win a raffle.
Scottish journalist after Scotland failed to qualify in 1970

Happiness is not having lost your last game.
Michel Platini

I think maybe it was a pity for French sport as a whole that Baron de Coubertin was one of us, a Frenchman, with his words about taking part being more important than winning.
Michel Platini on the new competitive spirit in French football

I can't go anywhere without someone coming up and telling me what I should have done.
Bobby Robson

ROBSON MUST GO.
Daily Mirror headline, shortly before tour of Mexico in which Robson's England team beat Brazil 2–0

He's a bit uptight. Criticism shouldn't affect him like it does. In his job you need a bloody thick skin.
Jack Charlton on Bobby Robson

He stands out as an honest man. That's what he is. Decent, hardworking and truthful.
Lawrie McMenemy on Bobby Robson

I find that if I have a go at them on a one-for-one basis very few can take it. They just can't take the criticism they shovel out in bucketfuls.
Bobby Robson on the British Press

Bobby Robson in front of (rather than over) the Pyramid of the Moon at Teotihuacan in Mexico

How many referees will give a penalty against a home team early in a match, when play is often most fierce?
Sir Stanley Rous

Me – hee – co. Ra – ra – ra.
Mexican supporters, 1970

Animals.
Alf Ramsey on the Argentina team after the quarter-final in England in 1966 during which Antonio Rattin was sent off

Try telling Pat Jennings it was fixed.
Billy Bingham, Northern Ireland manager, on his goalkeeper's vintage performance, after the 0–0 draw with England that Romania claimed was pre-arranged

The ball comes much faster, more unexpectedly than it does at sea level and it's not sure to stay true. Sometimes it's going all over the place. Things I'd eat up at home I may find myself really scrambling to hold. It may be safer at times to push them away and the lads will have to be ready for that situation.
Gordon Banks, on keeping goal at altitude

Anyone who could describe it as mild would be likely to tell you that hell is a good place for getting brown.
Hugh McIlvanney on the locals' descriptions of Guadalajara as 'mild and dry'

It is impossible for a European team to play more than an hour's football at top pressure here. The heat is terrible.
Mircea Lucescu, then captain of Romania, in 1970

Somebody's going to have to come up with something sensational for us.
Gerry Armstrong, hero of Valencia in '82, commenting ruefully on Northern Ireland's draw with Brazil, Spain and Algeria

Spain '82: N.Ireland's goalscoring hero Gerry Armstrong cuddles Billy Bingham after the historic win over Spain

We hardly knew his name beforehand so how could we have been afraid of him?
Finland manager Martti Kuusela on accusations that his players were frightened of Mark Hateley

Mark Hateley (England) poses in Mexico City on England's summer '85 tour. Maybe the guards are there to keep marauding hands off his shorts

We know the West Germans. We see them every week on television. They play machine football.
Sepp Piontek, manager of Denmark, on his first-round opponents

My old man said, 'You've got all your life after 35 to smoke, drink or go with women.' That's what I believe. I love football. If I am lucky enough to play against Brazil my old man will cry. And maybe I won't be far behind him. Me out there with Pele and those fellas. I'll say, 'This is the big time, Ballie. This is it, man, this is it.'
Alan Ball, 1970

I knew we were in bother when I spoke to Tommy Wright as he came in after the first match. I asked him if it were hard out there. He tried to speak but all he could do were keep swallowing. There was all white flecks round his mouth and his eyes was rolling. After about 15 or 20 seconds he said, 'F ★ ★ ★ ★ ★ hard.' And it were. You know Alan Mullery, always shouts at us. Go here, go there. He's a great worker and he drives you on. Well when he tried that out there all that came out was this sort of gurgle. Nobody had enough breath to run, let alone shout. I thought the talk about altitude was crap, me. I thought I could run for a week. But I found out different today.'
Alan Ball on the delights of playing in Mexico, 1970

Alan Ball, now manager of Portsmouth, once the engine room of England

I found a noticeable difference at first, especially balls being played to the chest. I found it bouncing away. The ball seems to be so damned lively as well, quite apart from the velocity, just like cricketers playing soft and hard wickets.
Geoff Hurst on the effects of playing at altitude

I am not an ice cube. If you are firing me, you had better say so. Don't hide behind words.
Joao Saldanho, manager of Brazil's 1970 team, on being told that the technical committee in charge of the World Cup challenge was being 'dissolved'

Football is very different from boxing. Its beauty is not burdened with the same physical and indivisibly personal penalties. Defeats for the most part bring only psychological suffering (the financial loss is rarely important to the players) and even that can be shared among eleven men. Yet at its highest levels the game can acquire something akin to the concentrated drama of the prize ring. Players go into some matches with the certain knowledge that the result will stay with them, however submerged, for the rest of their lives. Defeat will deposit a small, ineradicable sediment, just as victory will leave a few tiny bubbles of pleasure that can never quite disappear.
Arthur Hopcraft and Hugh McIlvanney, writing in World Cup '70 *on the game between Brazil and England in Guadalajara, won by Brazil 1–0*

Mexico has enough visible wretchedness to keep it on the underdeveloped list, even if mention of the fact gives bitter offence to its politicians. Is it not a moral affront to transport such a costly, frivolous show as the World Cup to such a place of need?
Arthur Hopcraft and Hugh McIlvanney, 1970

Mexico, with its heat and height, each of which placed such a dire burden on the competitors in 1970, gets the World Cup finals again, a mere 16 years later. Why?
Brian Glanville

We lost the World Cup – but it was still the finest England team I've played in.
Alan Ball, 1970

It's easy to beat Brazil. You just stop them getting 20 yards from your goal.
Bobby Charlton

Captured in time – a brilliant (and hirsute) Bobby Charlton

They used to say I was fat. Now they say I'm powerful.
Jan Molby, Liverpool and Denmark

Before the World Cup finals of 1978 a Lanarkshire bookmaker called Jim Tait launched a delightful and brilliantly sustained piece of nonsense about transporting a commando unit of the Tartan Army to Argentina in a converted U-boat. What Mr Tait couldn't know was that thousands of his countrymen would make the trip by hot-air balloon.
Hugh McIlvanney

I want every team that visits here to feel distinct fear when they get off the plane because they will know the Australian team eat raw meat. They are mad dogs and I am madder than the rest of them.
Frank Arok, manager of Australia, beaten for a place in the finals by Scotland

Leader of the mad dogs – Frank Arok of Australia

I know that if we win, some of our people are going to say, 'We have beaten the world.' I hate that. I will not have beaten the world. Eleven German footballers will have won a cup and I will be glad to see it. But I am not saying *I* have beaten anybody.
Ulrich Kaiser, West German journalist, before 1966 final

In the old days we used to go on field and play 'not to lose'. Now we go out onto the field and play to win. The difference is enormous. The importance is not winning, it is *wanting* to win.
Michel Hidalgo, former manager of France

TRAVEL TIPS

BEFORE YOU GO

A **Tourist Card** (valid up to 90 days) is the main entry requirement. If you're a British subject, go to the Mexican Consulate at 5 Halkin Street, London SW1 (01-253 6393) or the Mexican Tourist Office at 7 Cork Street, London W1 where you should be able to get one on the spot. By post takes longer. They will need passport details of the number, date of issue and date of expiry and it will cost you nothing.

A **US Visa** from the US Embassy at 5 Upper Grosvenor Street, London W1 (01-499 3443) is useful though not essential if you're flying – delays at airports can be tedious unless you can nip out for a cup of coffee. You will have to have one if you get off the plane at New York and bus, train or drive from there. Brave the mega-queues at the Embassy rather than apply by post, which takes ages.

Money: Travellers' cheques from one of the big-name companies (e.g. American Express, Thomas Cook) are your best bet, and all the major credit cards are accepted, though (bad for neurotic have-I-still-got-them pocket-patters) you do have the hassle of keeping tabs on them at all times. In some places, dollars are readily accepted as currency along with pesos. Dollars are also easy to change at banks throughout the country, and in big tourist areas most hotels, shops and restaurants will also oblige. Other currencies are harder to change so make it easy on yourself – don't roll up with a wallet full of guilder.

GETTING THERE

Plane: Continental Airlines are the big carriers to Mexico, mainly from the States, though they also do a London-Houston flight. This, taking advantage of an Apex fare, High Season rate, will work out around £587–£610 return inclusive of a connecting flight from Houston to Mexico City, Monterrey, Porto Vallarto, Acapulco, Cancun or Cozmunel. Your stay has to be a minimum of 7 days and a maximum of 60, so you must hope your team doesn't get knocked out in the first round. You *can* change your ticket locally for $50 but it's subject to space – which around World Cup time will probably be a problem.

You can also fly Concorde to Miami and on from there to Mexico City which will set you back £3,200 in all...

Bus: You can shop around the bucket shops, but the most straightforward way is Virgin Airlines to New York and Greyhound or Trailways from there. It's about two and a half days to the Mexican border. Once inside the country, the Mexican bus service is cheap, regular and efficient, both between major cities and even tiny villages (the latter service tends not to offer *tout confort,* of course). A good road map and a knowledge of Spanish helps, particularly when trying to cope in the hurly-burly of the ticket office.

Hitching: Plenty of young Americans backpack over the border into Mexico so you won't lack company. However, there are a few points to bear in mind. Firstly, it helps to have a reasonable command of the language as, outside most hotels and major cities, you won't find many people who speak English. Second, Mexico is a big place and a lot of it, particularly up north where Monterrey is situated, is deserted and barren, so you could well fetch up at some obscure roadside with an awful lot of time to kill between lifts. Third, drivers may ask you to chip in with a contribution towards expenses. Fourth, if you come over the border in a car your Tourist Card will be so marked and you may find yourself having to talk your way out of that when you leave the country again (see CAR section).

The best solution is to use hitching as a back-up over short distances, not only getting between cities to stadia in the same group, but also when you want to meet the people and see the life out (but not too far out) of town, have the resources to return to base in case of difficulty, and own a good set of maps.

Car (and Trailer): Taking a car and trailer, and sleeping rough, boils down to common sense. Most Mexicans will be really glad to see you, but stay out of the rough areas just as you would anywhere else in the world. Probably the worst risk to your bouncing good health is the food sold at some of the roadside stalls (all hitchers and bus-travellers take note, too).

If you have an accident, it's best to do a deal with the other motorist involved rather than call in the police (see below). Never witness an accident as there's a possibility of your getting locked up along with the defendants to prevent you going home before the case comes up.

Car hire will avoid most of these drawbacks and is no problem in Mexico, where most of the big name hire firms operate. Driving itself is very pleasant (if at times interestingly rustic) *away from Mexico City*. Everyone who has ever driven there has a horror story to tell – of 24-hour traffic jams, the locals' hairy driving style, the impossibility of getting spare parts for anything more recherché than a Ford or VW should you break down, the lack of parking places and risk of car theft. However, all this is as nought compared to your problems with the police force, who are probably going to nail you for at least one offence, real or imagined. (In either case the best bet is to plead ignorance and cough up whatever fine they ask.)

You *don't* need an international driving licence – a British one will do. You *do* need a Mexican insurance policy (obtainable at every border post), and your Tourist Card will be a special one to make sure you don't leave the car behind when you go (you aren't allowed to sell it and are responsible for taking the mangled wreckage home with you if you crash).

You *can* leave your car at one of the car parks found in all the US border towns (cheap rates for long-term storage) and continue by public transport, though then you sacrifice the biggest freedom of all – going where and when you please in Mexico.

Train: US trains aren't that interesting, but once over the border it's a better story. Some Mexican lines have improved significantly; the best by a mile is Chihuahua–Los Mochis in the north, which runs through amazing scenery and some spectacular feats of engineering. England supporters in Monterrey should try and ride on this, if they go nowhere else.

Going long distance is no problem. The sleepers are slow but reliable; you can take one (with a restaurant car) from the border to Mexico City. The cheapest sleepers are just carriages with bunks and curtains to draw round them, but if you've got cash to spare it's best to go for a *camarin* (a private compartment which holds one or two), or an *alcoba* (enough room for two adults and two kids, with its own washroom).

If you're travelling long distance on any other train, try and go first class – unless you enjoy sharing your personal space with goats, peasants, funny baggage, etc., on a long-term basis. A nice touch on Mexican trains is the stops they make for food vendors to board – winsome kids will sell you Coke and Hershey bars, and you can also get traditional snacks like tacos. All in all, a good way to see Mexico and indulge in your Clint Eastwood fantasies at the same time.

BEING THERE

Hotels and Food: Those of you who came in on Concorde will either be staying privately with the nobs or will be putting up at one of the luxury hotels in the Camino Real chain (there are three in Mexico City, one of which is the FIFA headquarters). In Acapulco, Hotel Las Brisas has 250 swimming pools (your own personal one, or shared with the room next door if you're really slumming it). It's obviously none too cheap, but when you get bored you can always look over the other side of the bay and watch Tom Jones's villa.

The earthquake damage in Mexico City has definitely been exaggerated by the press and in any case a great deal has already been done to put the city back together again. By the time the World Cup takes place, there will probably be few visible scars. Outside Mexico City, the only resort affected was Ixtapa, where a few hotels suffered damage.

Camping around the Mexico City area is not a very good idea. Once the World Cup is due to start (this applies to other venues too) there will be all sorts of accommodation available. There is also a case for going on spec and fixing up something when you're there because by that time the inevitable shortfall in demand will have shown up and prices will be lower.

Go for the cheaper local hotels at £7–£10 a night and sleep but don't eat. With the continuing devaluation of the peso, you can get a full 2-egg English breakfast in one of the 5-star hotels for around £2. There are some very good restaurants in Mexico City and the other venues, most of which are attached to hotels, and which provide international cooking as well as Mexican if you don't want to eat hot and spicy. There are also numerous fast-food enterprises and interesting one-owner places. You won't eat anywhere which looks dirty, will you?

Police: Mexico is very Americanised (it deals with three and a half million tourists a year) so it is very geared up to the occasion, more than most people have appreciated. But *don't* cross the law because they're very hard on people and will not be amused if you get plastered and jump into the fountains in the middle of the main drag. Traffic 'offences' are often punished by on the spot fines or removal of your number plates (especially if you argue with them), and it will cost you a bomb to buy them back. Mexicans call it *la mordida* – the bite. If you get into any other kind of trouble with the police, it is quite in order to try bribing them.

What to take: Mexico tends to dress very casually, so short sleeves and smart trousers/skirts will get you through most social occasions. Unless you intend to get presented to Joao Havelange, the President of FIFA, or the local Queen of the May, there is no need to burden yourself with a black tie and tails or a backless gown. What you will need is a good suntan oil. Monterrey will be really hot and to follow England in comfort take a good pair of sunglasses and a hat or cap for sitting in the stadium in the sun. The rainy season is around, so also take a light waterproof anorak/pacamac.

Health: Go equipped with loo paper, insect repellent, your usual brand of pain-killers (e.g. paracetamol) and some anti-poo pills. Anything else you need will probably be obtainable from the chemist over there (look out for a big green cross and the name *Farmacia*). Before you go, a cholera/typhoid inoculation is a sensible precaution. Make sure, too, that your polio and tetanus boosters are up to date.

Do take out a good **travel insurance policy,** which for around £10 a month will cover you for basic medical problems as well as mishaps such as theft. You can get one from an insurance broker or your travel agent.

If the worst comes to the worst, Mexican hospitals are very good. There are also plenty of English-speaking doctors – get a list from the nearest British or US Consulate.

Your main health problem will no doubt be diarrhoea (the trots, grotty botty, Montezuma's revenge or whatever the family name is). The *Farmacia* is experienced in dispensing for this if necessary. You can go through the routine of Not Touching The Tap Water, Avoiding The Fruit And Raw Vegetables, etc., but you'll probably get something anyway. Common sense is to drink bottled water, check with the hotel that the drinking water really is what they say it is, and take it easy on the alcohol/spicy food front the first couple of days. Avoid Mexico's gruesome public loos, if only for aesthetic reasons.

Telephoning home will be expensive. You can make international calls from anywhere with a sign saying *Larga Distancia* (in bus and railway stations as well as most Telefonos offices). At these, your call is logged on a meter by the operator who will then give you the bill. You may be able to dial direct at your hotel but it will cost you.

Drink the tequila (it can be pretty hairy on its own but the Margaritas are wonderful). Mexican beer is excellent and there are lots of good varieties. Wine – go for the Mexico reds, notably the Pedro Domecq label.

Buy the arts and crafts. Silver is very reasonably priced. Bartering in markets is very common, and possibly in small shops, but *never* in a department store. Bartering is a knack like any other. Try pointing to an object and asking, 'Is this the best price?' Vendors are usually resigned to the fact that a few pesos are going to be knocked off the final bill. Don't appear very interested, and as a last resort walk away – it's a traditional tactic that still works.

What to see: As many of the spectacular sights as you can, of course. Arm yourself with a good guide book (the Fodor is reliable, and for travellers on a budget, *The Rough Guide to Mexico* by John Fisher) before you go; this is just intended as a brief rundown.

Mexico is a very ancient civilisation (Aztec, Mayan), with influences of sixteenth-century Spanish. *Mexico City* was a fourteenth-/fifteenth-century Aztec capital. Outside the boundaries are the Pyramids of Teotihuacan, a miraculous archeological site, and Mexico's Lourdes, the shrine of Guadalupe. For those with time and money to spare, Oaxaca (an Indian and Colonial city) is 45 minutes away by plane. Go also to Villahermosa (museums and the Mayan ruins of Palenque in the rain forest). There are also Mayan sites near Merida, Uxmal and Chichen Itza.

Around *Monterrey* is where Pancho Villa roamed in times of revolution. Bogart fans can explore the Sierra Madre. This is where to take the train through the Copper Canyon, which makes the Grand Canyon look like a crack in the pavement. *Acapulco* is nirvana for those who like beaches, bars, discos and bright lights, and who have good enough constitutions to cope with the consequences.

WHAT TO SAY

It is to be hoped that you will not need to memorise the phrases issued in an NUJ handbook to unlucky hacks covering the '78 World Cup in Argentina. These included *Dejen de torturarme, por favor* (Please stop torturing me), *Mi periodico les pagara bien si me dejen ir* (My newspaper will pay well if you let me go), and *Por favor entregen mi cuerpo a mi familia* (Please deliver my body to my family).

The following guide to Spanish pronunciation and useful phrases should be all you need for less traumatic occasions:

Spanish is not only a simple language to learn and pronounce but also one of the most mellifluous sounding. Just a smattering will earn you Brownie points with the nationals in Mexico.

Mexican Spanish is almost identical to Castilian Spanish, with one or two variations in pronunciation. In Castilian, C is pronounced as Th before E and I, and as K before A, O and U – unless there is a little sign called a *cedilla* underneath it which will make the C look like this: Ç. Any Ç is pronounced Th and the obvious example is Barcelona Football Club, whose nickname is Barça. In Mexican Spanish, a similar format applies, except that the soft C is pronounced not as Th but S.

D is a bit softer than in English;
shape your mouth to say *The* when you say it.

G is similar to C in that it is soft before E and I, and a rather guttural sound – as though you're saying *Hog* with your mouth shaped to say *Kog*. Before A, O and U it is pronounced as in *garage, gone* and *gullible. Gui* is pronounced as one syllable, as in *McGhee* rather than as *gooey. Gue* is pronounced as in *guerilla*.

H is silent, as in French.

J is, for all intents and purposes, the same as G.

Ll is like the English Y in *yoke, Yukon* or *Yorick*.

N is as in English (*nose, nuts, nefarious*) unless it has a little sign called a *tilde* over the top. N with a *tilde* over it looks like this – Ñ or ñ – and is pronounced *nye* as in *neuralgia, onion*, and *mañana*.

Qu is the Spanish equivalent of the English K.

S is a bit more hissy and lispy in Spanish, as though you purse your lips to say *soap* while making the sound *thoap*.

In Spanish, you rrroll your RRRs. T is similar to English T but a bit more staccato and hard. When you say V give it a dash of B, and when you say B give it a touch of V.

X is pronounced as an aspirate, as in Me–hee–co.

Z is a Th sound in Castilian Spanish, and an S sound in Mexican.

A – as in *Malaga* or *bandit* but not *facial* or *racist*.

E – as in *elementary* or *et cetera* but not *evil* or *Eeyore*.

I – as in *terrine* or *caprice* but not *island* or *ivy*.

O – as in *columbine* or *dromedary* but not *go-go* or *snowman*.

U – as in *lupin* or *Rubik* but not *umbrella* or *mullet*.

DAYS OF THE WEEK

(stress the syllable underlined)

Monday	*lunes*
Tuesday	*martes*
Wednesday	*miercoles*
Thursday	*jueves*
Friday	*viernes*
Saturday	*sabado*
Sunday	*domingo*

NUMBERS

1	*uno* (or *una* in the feminine gender)
2	*dos*
3	*tres*
4	*cuatro*
5	*cinco*
6	*seis*
7	*siete*
8	*ocho*
9	*nueve*
10	*diez*
11	*once*
12	*doce*
13	*trece*
14	*catorce*
15	*quince*
16	*diez y seis*
17	*diez y siete*
18	*diez y ocho*
19	*diez y nueve*
20	*veinte* (pronounced *bente)*
21	*veintiuno*
30	*treinta*
40	*cuarenta*
50	*cincuenta*
60	*sesenta*
70	*setenta*
80	*ochenta*
90	*noventa*
100	*cien*
200	*doscientos*
500	*quinientos*
700	*setecientos*
1000	*mil*
2000	*dos mil*

BREAD AND BUTTER WORDS

Yes	*si*
No	*no*
Please	*por favor*
Thank you	*gracias*
With	*con*
Without	*sin*
Still water	*agua sin gas*
Fizzy water	*agua con gas*
Good	*buen* (on its own, *bueno* or *buena* with a noun or describing something with a known gender)
Bad	*mal (malo/mala)*
Less	*menos*
This	*esto*
That	*eso*
Now	*ahora*
After	*despues (de)*
Later	*mas tarde* (literally, more late)
Here	*aqui*
There	*alla*
Today	*hoy*
Tomorrow	*mañana*
Yesterday	*ayer*
When	*cuando*
What	*que*
How much	*cuanto*
Where	*donde* (Where is . . .? *donde esta . . .?*)
Big	*gran, grande*
Small	*pequeño(a)*
Open	*abierto*
Closed	*cerrado*
Hallo	*hola*
Good morning	*buenos dias*
Good afternoon	*buenas tardes*
Goodnight	*buenas noches*
Goodbye	*adios*
Sorry	*lo siento*
Excuse me	*perdon*
You're welcome	*de nada*
I don't understand	*no entiendo*
Do you speak English?	*habla ingles?*
What's your name?	*como se llama?* (literally, How are you called?)

My name is . . .	*me llamo*
Exit	*salida*
Entrance	*entrada*
Other	*otro/otra*
I'd like	*quiero/quisiera*
Have you . . .?	
(do you have . . .?)	*tiene usted . . .?*
Do you know . . .?	*sabe usted?*
I don't know	*no se*
	(pronounced say)
Can I . . .? (Is it	
possible to . . .?)	*se puede . . .?*
What is the time?	*que hora es?*

FOOD BASICS

Bread	*pan*
Wine	*vino*
Beer	*cerveza*
Butter	*mantequilla*
Red wine	*tinto*
Water	*agua*
Rice	*arroz*
Soup	*sopa*
Hors d'oeuvres	*entremeses*
Fish	*pescado*
Cheese	*queso*
Eggs	*huevos*
Meat	*carne*
Salt	*sal*
Pepper	*pimienta*
Sauce	*salsa*
Ham	*jamon*
Milk	*leche*
Pork	*cerdo*
Lamb	*cordero*
Rabbit	*conejo*
Chicken	*pollo*
Sausage	*butifarra/*
	salchicha
Veal	*ternera*
Anchovies	*anchoas*
Tuna	*atun*
Hake	*merluza*
Prawns	*camarones*
Avocado	*aguacate*
Peach	*melocoton*

Orange	*naranja*
Banana	*platano*
Beans	*frijoles*
Onion	*cebolla*
Baked	*al horno*
Grilled	*parillada*
Roast	*asado*

TRAVELLING

Airport	*aeropuerto*
Train	*tren*
Aeroplane	*avion/aeroplano*
Centre	*centro*
Summer	*verano*
Car	*coche*
Bus	*camion*
Hotel	*hotel*
North	*norte*
City	*ciudad*
Station	*estacion*
Street	*calle*
Square	*plaza*
House	*casa*
Timetable	*horario*
Ticket	*billete*
Money	*dinero*
Passenger	*pasajero*
Newspaper	*periodico*
Buy	*comprar*
Smoke	*fumar*
Change	*cambiar*
Wait	*esperar*
Travel	*viajar*
Luggage	*equipaje*
Railways	*ferrocarril*

USEFUL PHRASES

I want to buy a ticket
Quiero comprar una billete/una entrada

What time is kick-off?
A que hora empieze el partido?

Does this bus go to the stadium?
to the city centre?
Va este camion al estadio?
al centro ciudad?

You are sitting in my seat
Esta en mi asiento

Where can I telephone?
Donde esta un telefono?

May I have the bill, please?
La cuenta, por favor

I'd like to go to the stadium/
the station/the hotel/the airport
Quisiera ir al estadio/a la estacion/
al hotel/ al aeropuerto

What are you eating/drinking?
Que come usted/que bebe usted

I'm looking for a hotel
Busco un hotel

Where do you live?
Donde habita usted?

I have to . . .
Tengo que . . .

Do you have a comfortable room?
Tiene usted un dormitorio comodo?

I am very hot
Tengo mucho calor

I am on holiday
Estoy de vacaciones

What are you doing after the game?
Que hace usted despues del partido?

When are England playing?
Cuando juegan Inglaterra?

Do you play football?
Juega usted al futbol?

Where is my luggage?
Donde esta mi equipaje?

I am staying in this hotel
Paro en este hotel

I don't have much money
No tengo mucho dinero

I'd like to see the city sights
Quiero ir a ver las cosas de interes
de la ciudad

I think that . . .
Me parece que . . .

Bring me a coffee
Me traiga usted en cafe

It's one o'clock/two o'clock/
half past three/five fifteen/
quarter to one
Es la una/son las dos/
son las tres y media/
son las cinco y cuartro/
son las una menos cuarto

Seven o'clock in the morning/
in the evening
Las siete de la mañana/de la tarde

The seven o'clock train
El tren de las siete

What is the date?
A cuantos estamos?

That's it/that's right
Eso es

Here is my ticket
Aqui esta mi billete/entrada

Which seats?
Que asientos?

The first/second/third/fourth/fifth/ sixth/
seventh/eighth/ninth/tenth row
(After 10th use the cardinal number,
e.g. row eleven, *la fila once*)
La primera/segunda/tercera/cuarta/
quinta/sexta/septima/octava/novena/
decima fila

I don't understand
No comprendo

I don't know anyone
No conozco a nadie

Which of these seats do you want?
Cual de estos asientos desea usted?

Which players do you like?
Cuales de las jugadores le gustan a usted?

I like (singular/plural)
Me gusta . . ./gustan . . .

I don't like . . .
No me gusta . . .

WORLD CUP FINALS 1930-1982

URUGUAY 1930

POOL 1

		P	W	D	L	F	A	Pts
France 4, Mexico 1	Argentina	3	3	0	0	10	4	6
Argentina 1, France 0	Chile	3	2	0	1	5	3	4
Chile 3, Mexico 0	France	3	1	0	2	4	3	2
Chile 1, France 0	Mexico	3	0	0	3	4	13	0
Argentina 6, Mexico 3								
Argentina 3, Chile 1								

POOL 2

		P	W	D	L	F	A	Pts
Yugoslavia 2, Brazil 1	Yugoslavia	2	2	0	0	6	1	4
Yugoslavia 4, Bolivia 0	Brazil	2	1	0	1	5	2	2
Brazil 4, Bolivia 0	Bolivia	2	0	0	2	0	8	0

POOL 3

		P	W	D	L	F	A	Pts
Romania 3, Peru 1	Uruguay	2	2	0	0	5	0	4
Uruguay 1, Peru 0	Romania	2	1	0	1	3	5	2
Uruguay 4, Romania 0	Peru	2	0	0	2	1	4	0

POOL 4

		P	W	D	L	F	A	Pts
United States 3, Belgium 0	United States	2	2	0	0	6	0	4
United States 3, Paraguay 0	Paraguay	2	1	0	1	1	3	2
Paraguay 1, Belgium 0	Belgium	2	0	0	2	0	4	0

SEMI-FINALS
Argentina 6, United States 1
Uruguay 6, Yugoslavia 1

FINAL *Montevideo*
Uruguay 4, Argentina 2

Uruguay: Ballesteros, Nasazzi (capt.), Mascheroni, Andrade, Fernandez, Gestido, Dorado, Scarone, Castro, Cea, Iriarte.

Argentina: Botasso, Della Torre, Paternoster, Evaristo J., Monti, Suarez, Peucelle, Varallo, Stabile, Ferreira (capt.), Evaristo M.

Scorers: Dorado, Cea, Iriarte, Castro for Uruguay; Peucelle, Stabile for Argentina.

Leading Scorer: Stabile (Argentina) 8.

ITALY 1934

FIRST ROUND
Italy 7, United States 1
Czechoslovakia 2, Romania 1
Germany 5, Belgium 2
Austria 3, France 2
Spain 3, Brazil 1
Switzerland 3, Holland 2
Sweden 3, Argentina 2
Hungary 4, Egypt 2

SECOND ROUND
Germany 2, Sweden 1
Austria 2, Hungary 1
Italy 1, Spain 1
Italy 1, Spain 0 *replay*
Czechoslovakia 3, Switzerland 2

SEMI-FINALS
Czechoslovakia 3, Germany 1
Italy 1, Austria 0

THIRD PLACE MATCH
Germany 3, Austria 2

FINAL *Rome*
Italy 2, Czechoslovakia 1 after extra time.

Italy Combi (capt.), Monzeglio, Allemandi, Ferraris IV, Monti, Bertolini, Guaita, Meazza, Schiavio, Ferrari, Orsi.

Czechoslovakia: Planicka (capt.), Zenisek, Ctyroky, Kostalek, Cambal, Krcil, Junek, Svoboda, Sobotka, Nejedly, Puc.

Scorers: Orsi, Schiavio for Italy; Puc for Czechoslovakia.

Leading Scovers: Schiavio (Italy), Nejedly (Czechoslovakia), Conen (Germany) each 4.

FRANCE 1938

FIRST ROUND
Switzerland 1, Germany 1
Switzerland 4, Germany 2 *replay*
Cuba 3, Romania 3
Cuba 2, Romania 1 *replay*
Hungary 6, Dutch East Indies 0
France 3, Belgium 1
Czechoslovakia 3, Holland 0
Brazil 6, Poland 5
Italy 2, Norway 1

SECOND ROUND
Sweden 8, Cuba 0
Hungary 2, Switzerland 0
Italy 3, France 1
Brazil 1, Czechoslovakia 1
Brazil 2, Czechoslovakia 1 *replay*

SEMI-FINALS
Italy 2, Brazil 1
Hungary 5, Sweden 1

THIRD PLACE MATCH
Brazil 4, Sweden 2

FINAL *Paris*
Italy 4, Hungary 2

Italy: Olivieri, Foni, Rava, Serantoni, Andreolo, Locatelli, Biavati, Meazza (capt.), Piola, Ferrari, Colaussi.

Hungary: Szabo, Polgar, Biro, Szalay, Szucs, Lazar, Sas, Vincze, Sarosi (capt.), Szengeller, Titkos.

Scorers: Colaussi (2), Piola (2) for Italy; Titkos, Sarosi for Hungary.

Leading Scorer: Leonidas (Brazil) 8.

BRAZIL 1950

POOL 1

Brazil 4, Mexico 0
Yugoslavia 3, Switzerland 0
Yugoslavia 4, Mexico 1
Brazil 2, Switzerland 2
Brazil 2, Yugoslavia 0
Switzerland 2, Mexico 1

	P	W	D	L	F	A	Pts
Brazil	3	2	1	0	8	2	5
Yugoslavia	3	2	0	1	7	3	4
Switzerland	3	1	1	1	4	6	3
Mexico	3	0	0	3	2	10	0

POOL 2

Spain 3, United States 1
England 2, Chile 0
United States 1, England 0
Spain 2, Chile 0
Spain 1, England 0
Chile 5, United States 2

	P	W	D	L	F	A	Pts
Spain	3	3	0	0	6	1	6
England	3	1	0	2	2	2	2
Chile	3	1	0	2	5	6	2
United States	3	1	0	2	4	8	2

POOL 3

Sweden 3, Italy 2
Sweden 2 Paraguay 2
Italy 2, Paraguay 0

	P	W	D	L	F	A	Pts
Sweden	2	1	1	0	5	4	3
Italy	2	1	0	1	4	3	2
Paraguay	2	0	1	1	2	4	1

POOL 4

Uruguay 8, Bolivia 0

	P	W	D	L	F	A	Pts
Uruguay	1	1	0	0	8	0	2
Bolivia	1	0	0	1	0	8	0

Final pool replaced knock-out system.

FINAL POOL *São Paulo and Rio de Janeiro*

Uruguay 2, Spain 2
Brazil 7, Sweden 1
Uruguay 3, Sweden 2
Brazil 6, Spain 1
Sweden 3, Spain 1
Uruguay 2, Brazil 1

	P	W	D	L	F	A	Pts
Uruguay	3	2	1	0	7	5	5
Brazil	3	2	0	1	14	4	4
Sweden	3	1	0	2	6	11	2
Spain	3	0	1	2	4	11	1

Leading Scorers: Ademir (Brazil) 7, Schiaffino (Uruguay), Basora (Spain) 5.

SWITZERLAND 1954

GROUP 1

Yugoslavia 1, France 0
Brazil 5, Mexico 0
France 3, Mexico 2
Brazil 1, Yugoslavia 1

	P	W	D	L	F	A	Pts
Brazil	2	1	1	0	6	1	3
Yugoslavia	2	1	1	0	2	1	3
France	2	1	0	1	3	3	2
Mexico	2	0	0	2	2	8	0

GROUP 2

Hungary 9, Korea 0
W. Germany 4, Turkey 1
Hungary 8, W. Germany 3
Turkey 7, Korea 0

	P	W	D	L	F	A	Pts
Hungary	2	2	0	0	17	3	4
W. Germany	2	1	0	1	7	9	2
Turkey	2	1	0	1	8	4	2
Korea	2	0	0	2	0	16	0

PLAY-OFF MATCH

W. Germany 7, Turkey 2

GROUP 3

Austria 1, Scotland 0
Uruguay 2, Czechoslovakia 0
Austria 5, Czechoslovakia 0
Uruguay 7, Scotland 0

	P	W	D	L	F	A	Pts
Uruguay	2	2	0	0	9	0	4
Austria	2	2	0	0	6	0	4
Czechoslovakia	2	0	0	2	0	7	0
Scotland	2	0	0	2	0	8	0

GROUP 4

England 4, Belgium 4
England 2, Switzerland 0
Switzerland 2, Italy 1
Italy 4, Belgium 1

	P	W	D	L	F	A	Pts
England	2	1	1	0	6	4	3
Italy	2	1	0	1	5	3	2
Switzerland	2	1	0	1	2	3	2
Belgium	2	0	1	1	5	8	1

PLAY-OFF MATCH

Switzerland 4, Italy 1

QUARTER-FINALS

W. Germany 2, Yugoslavia 0
Hungary 4, Brazil 2
Austria 7, Switzerland 5
Uruguay 4, England 2

SEMI-FINALS

West Germany 6, Austria 1
Hungary 4, Uruguay 2

THIRD PLACE MATCH

Austria 3, Uruguay 1

FINAL *Berne*

West Germany 3, Hungary 2

West Germany: Turek, Posipal, Kohlmeyer, Eckel, Liebrich, Mai, Rahn, Morlock, Walter O., Walter F. (capt.), Schaefer.

Hungary: Grosics, Buzansky, Lantos, Bozsik, Lorant, Zakarias, Czibor, Kocsis, Hidegkuti, Puskas (capt.), Toth J.

Scorers: Morlock, Rahn (2) for Germany; Puskas, Czibor for Hungary.

Leading Scorer: Kocsis (Hungary) 11.

SWEDEN 1958

GROUP 1

W. Germany 3, Argentina 1
N. Ireland 1, Czechoslovakia 0
W. Germany 2, Czechoslovakia 2
Argentina 3, N. Ireland 1
W. Germany 2, N. Ireland 2
Czechoslovakia 6, Argentina 1

	P	W	D	L	F	A	Pts
West Germany	3	1	2	0	7	5	4
Czechoslovakia	3	1	1	1	8	4	3
N. Ireland	3	1	1	1	4	5	3
Argentina	3	1	0	2	5	10	2

PLAY-OFF MATCH
N. Ireland 2, Czechoslovakia 1

GROUP 2

France 7, Paraguay 3
Yugoslavia 1, Scotland 1
Yugoslavia 3, France 2
Paraguay 3, Scotland 2
France 2, Scotland 1
Yugoslavia 3, Paraguay 3

	P	W	D	L	F	A	Pts
France	3	2	0	1	11	7	4
Yugoslavia	3	1	2	0	7	6	4
Paraguay	3	1	1	1	9	12	3
Scotland	3	0	1	2	4	6	1

GROUP 3

Sweden 3, Mexico 0
Hungary 1, Wales 1
Wales 1, Mexico 1
Sweden 2, Hungary 1
Sweden 0, Wales 0
Hungary 4, Mexico 0

	P	W	D	L	F	A	Pts
Sweden	3	2	1	0	5	1	5
Hungary	3	1	1	1	6	3	3
Wales	3	0	3	0	2	2	3
Mexico	3	0	1	2	1	8	1

PLAY-OFF MATCH

Wales 2, Hungary 1

GROUP 4

England 2, Russia 2
Brazil 3, Austria 0
England 0, Brazil 0
Russia 2, Austria 0
Brazil 2, Russia 0
England 2, Austria 2

	P	W	D	L	F	A	Pts
Brazil	3	2	1	0	5	0	5
England	3	0	3	0	4	4	3
Russia	3	1	1	1	4	4	3
Austria	3	0	1	2	2	7	1

PLAY-OFF MATCH
Russia 1, England 0

QUARTER-FINALS
France 4, N. Ireland 0
W. Germany 1, Yugoslavia 0
Sweden 2, Russia 0
Brazil 1, Wales 0

SEMI-FINALS
Brazil 5, France 2
Sweden 3, West Germany 1

THIRD PLACE MATCH
France 6, West Germany 3

FINAL *Stockholm*
Brazil 5, Sweden 2

Brazil: Gilmar, Santos D., Santos N., Zito, Bellini, Orlando, Garrincha, Didi, Vava, Pele, Zagalo.
Sweden: Svensson, Bergmark, Axbom, Boerjesson, Gustavsson, Parling, Hamrin, Gren, Simonsson, Liedholm, Skoglund.
Scorers: Vava (2), Pele (2), Zagalo for Brazil; Liedholm, Simonsson for Sweden.
Leading Scorer: Fontaine (France) 13 (present record total).

CHILE 1962

GROUP 1

Uruguay 2, Colombia 1
Russia 2, Yugoslavia 0
Yugoslavia 3, Uruguay 1
Russia 4, Colombia 4
Russia 2, Uruguay 1
Yugoslavia 5, Colombia 0

	P	W	D	L	F	A	Pts
Russia	3	2	1	0	8	5	5
Yugoslavia	3	2	0	1	8	3	4
Uruguay	3	1	0	2	4	6	2
Colombia	3	0	1	2	5	11	1

GROUP 2

Chile 3, Switzerland 1
W. Germany 0, Italy 0
Chile 2, Italy 0
W. Germany 2, Switzerland 1
W. Germany 2, Chile 0
Italy 3, Switzerland 0

	P	W	D	L	F	A	Pts
W. Germany	3	2	1	0	4	1	5
Chile	3	2	0	1	5	2	4
Italy	3	1	1	1	3	2	3
Switzerland	3	0	0	3	2	8	0

GROUP 3

Brazil 2, Mexico 0
Czechoslovakia 1, Spain 0
Brazil 0, Czechoslovakia 0
Spain 1, Mexico 0
Brazil 2, Spain 1
Mexico 3, Czechoslovakia 1

	P	W	D	L	F	A	Pts
Brazil	3	2	1	0	4	1	5
Czechoslovakia	3	1	1	1	2	3	3
Mexico	3	1	0	2	3	4	2
Spain	3	1	0	2	2	3	2

GROUP 4

Argentina 1, Bulgaria 0
Hungary 2, England 1
England 3, Argentina 1
Hungary 6, Bulgaria 1
Argentina 0, Hungary 0
England 0, Bulgaria 0

	P	W	D	L	F	A	Pts
Hungary	3	2	1	0	8	2	5
England	3	1	1	1	4	3	3
Argentina	3	1	1	1	2	3	3
Bulgaria	3	0	1	2	1	7	1

QUARTER-FINALS

Yugoslavia 1, W. Germany 0
Brazil 3, England 1
Chile 2, Russia 1
Czechoslovakia 1, Hungary 0

SEMI-FINALS

Brazil 4, Chile 2
Czechoslovakia 3, Yugoslavia 1

THIRD PLACE MATCH

Chile 1, Yugoslavia 0

FINAL *Santiago*

Brazil 3, Czechoslovakia 1

Brazil: Gilmar, Santos D., Mauro, Zozimo, Santos N., Zito, Didi, Garrincha, Vava, Amarildo, Zagalo.

Czechoslovakia: Schroiff, Tichy, Novak, Pluskal, Popluhar, Masopust, Pospichal, Scherer, Kvasniak, Kadraba, Jelinek.

Scorers: Amarildo, Zito, Vava, for Brazil; Masopust for Czechoslovakia.

Leading Scorers: Albert (Hungary), Ivanov (Russia), Sanchez L. (Chile), Garrincha, Vava (Brazil), Jerkovic (Yugoslavia) each 4.

ENGLAND 1966

GROUP 1

England 0, Uruguay 0
France 1, Mexico 1
Uruguay 2, France 1
England 2, Mexico 0
Uruguay 0, Mexico 0
England 2, France 0

	P	W	D	L	F	A	Pts
England	3	2	1	0	4	0	5
Uruguay	3	1	2	0	2	1	4
Mexico	3	0	2	1	1	3	2
France	3	0	1	2	2	5	1

GROUP 2

W. Germany 5, Switzerland 0
Argentina 2, Spain 1
Spain 2, Switzerland 1
Argentina 0, W. Germany 0
Argentina 2, Switzerland 0
W. Germany 2, Spain 1

	P	W	D	L	F	A	Pts
West Germany	3	2	1	0	7	1	5
Argentina	3	2	1	0	4	1	5
Spain	3	1	0	2	4	5	2
Switzerland	3	0	0	3	1	9	0

GROUP 3

Brazil 2, Bulgaria 0
Portugal 3, Hungary 1
Hungary 3, Brazil 1
Portugal 3, Bulgaria 0
Portugal 3, Brazil 1
Hungary 3, Bulgaria 1

	P	W	D	L	F	A	Pts
Portugal	3	3	0	0	9	2	6
Hungary	3	2	0	1	7	5	4
Brazil	3	1	0	2	4	6	2
Bulgaria	3	0	0	3	1	8	0

GROUP 4

Russia 3, N. Korea 0
Italy 2, Chile 0
Chile 1, N. Korea 1
Russia 1, Italy 0
N. Korea 1, Italy 0
Russia 2, Chile 1

	P	W	D	L	F	A	Pts
Russia	3	3	0	0	6	1	6
N. Korea	3	1	1	1	2	4	3
Italy	3	1	0	2	2	2	2
Chile	3	0	1	2	2	5	1

QUARTER-FINALS

England 1, Argentina 0
West Germany 4, Uruguay 0
Portugal 5, North Korea 3
Russia 2, Hungary 1

SEMI-FINALS

West Germany 2, Russia 1
England 2, Portugal 1

THIRD PLACE MATCH

Portugal 2, Russia 1

FINAL *Wembley, London*
England 4, West Germany 2 after extra time

England: Banks, Cohen, Wilson, Stiles, Charlton J., Moore, Ball, Hurst, Hunt, Charlton R., Peters.

West Germany: Tilkowski, Hottges, Schulz, Weber, Schnellinger, Haller, Beckenbauer, Overath, Seeler, Held, Emmerich.

Scorers: Hurst (3), Peters for England; Haller, Weber for Germany.

Leading Scorer: Eusebio (Portugal) 9.

MEXICO 1970

GROUP A
Mexico 0, Russia 0
Belgium 3, El Salvador 0
Russia 4, Belgium 1
Mexico 4, El Salvador 0
Russia 2, El Salvador 0
Belgium 0, Mexico 1

	P	W	D	L	F	A	Pts
Russia	3	2	1	0	6	1	5
Mexico	3	2	1	0	5	0	5
Belgium	3	1	0	2	4	5	2
El Salvador	3	0	0	3	0	9	0

GROUP B
Uruguay 2, Israel 0
Italy 1, Sweden 0
Uruguay 0, Italy 0
Israel 1, Sweden 1
Sweden 1, Uruguay 0
Israel 0, Italy 0

	P	W	D	L	F	A	Pts
Italy	3	1	2	0	1	0	4
Uruguay	3	1	1	1	2	1	3
Sweden	3	1	1	1	2	2	3
Israel	3	0	2	1	1	3	2

GROUP C
England 1, Romania 0
Brazil 4, Czechoslovakia 1
Romania 2, Czechoslovakia 1
Brazil 1, England 0
Brazil 3, Romania 2
England 1, Czechoslovakia 0

	P	W	D	L	F	A	Pts
Brazil	3	3	0	0	8	3	6
England	3	2	0	1	2	1	4
Romania	3	1	0	2	4	5	2
Czechoslovakia	3	0	0	3	2	7	0

GROUP D
Peru 3, Bulgaria 2
W. Germany 2, Morocco 1
Peru 3, Morocco 0
W. Germany 5, Bulgaria 2
W. Germany 3, Peru 1
Bulgaria 1, Morocco 1

	P	W	D	L	F	A	Pts
W. Germany	3	3	0	0	10	4	6
Peru	3	2	0	1	7	5	4
Bulgaria	3	0	1	2	5	9	1
Morocco	3	0	1	2	2	6	1

QUARTER-FINALS
Uruguay 1, Russia 0
Italy 4, Mexico 1
Brazil 4, Peru 2
West Germany 3, England 2

SEMI-FINALS
Italy 4, West Germany 3
Brazil 3, Uruguay 1

THIRD PLACE MATCH
West Germany 1, Uruguay 0

FINAL *Mexico City*
Brazil 4, Italy 1

Brazil: Felix, Carlos Alberto, Brito, Piazza, Everaldo, Gerson, Clodoaldo, Jairzinho, Pele, Tostao, Rivelino. (No subs.)

Italy: Albertosi, Burgnich, Cera, Rosato, Facchetti, Bertini, Riva, Domenghini, Mazzola, De Sisti, Boninsegna. Subs: Juliano for Bertini, Rivera for Boninsegna.

Scorers: Pele, Gerson, Jairzinho, Carlos Alberto for Brazil; Boninsegna for Italy.

Leading Scorers: Muller (West Germany) 10.

WEST GERMANY 1974

GROUP 1

West Germany 1, Chile 0
East Germany 2, Australia 0
West Germany 3, Australia 0
East Germany 1, Chile 1
East Germany 1, West Germany 0
Chile 0, Australia 0

	P	W	D	L	F	A	Pts
East Germany	3	2	1	0	4	1	5
West Germany	3	2	0	1	4	1	4
Chile	3	0	2	1	1	2	2
Australia	3	0	1	2	0	5	1

GROUP 2

Brazil 0, Yugoslavia 0
Scotland 2, Zaire 0
Brazil 0, Scotland 0
Yugoslavia 9, Zaire 0
Scotland 1, Yugoslavia 1
Brazil 3, Zaire 0

	P	W	D	L	F	A	Pts
Yugoslavia	3	1	2	0	10	1	4
Brazil	3	1	2	0	3	0	4
Scotland	3	1	2	0	3	1	4
Zaire	3	0	0	3	0	14	0

GROUP 3

Holland 2, Uruguay 0
Sweden 0, Bulgaria 0
Holland 0, Sweden 0
Bulgaria 1, Uruguay 1
Holland 4, Bulgaria 1
Sweden 3, Uruguay 0

	P	W	D	L	F	A	Pts
Holland	3	2	1	0	6	1	5
Sweden	3	1	2	0	3	0	4
Bulgaria	3	0	2	1	2	5	2
Uruguay	3	0	1	2	1	6	1

GROUP 4

Italy 3, Haiti 1
Poland 3, Argentina 2
Argentina 1, Italy 1
Poland 7, Haiti 0
Argentina 4, Haiti 1
Poland 2, Italy 1

	P	W	D	L	F	A	Pts
Poland	3	3	0	0	12	3	6
Argentina	3	1	1	1	7	5	3
Italy	3	1	1	1	5	4	3
Haiti	3	0	0	3	2	14	0

GROUP A

Brazil 1, East Germany 0
Holland 4, Argentina 0
Holland 2, East Germany 0
Brazil 2, Argentina 1
Holland 2, Brazil 0
Argentina 1, East Germany 1

	P	W	D	L	F	A	Pts
Holland	3	3	0	0	8	0	6
Brazil	3	2	0	1	3	3	4
East Germany	3	0	1	2	1	4	1
Argentina	3	0	1	2	2	7	1

GROUP B

Poland 1, Sweden 0
West Germany 2, Yugoslavia 0
Poland 2, Yugoslavia 1
West Germany 4, Sweden 2
Sweden 2, Yugoslavia 1
West Germany 1, Poland 0

	P	W	D	L	F	A	Pts
West Germany	3	3	0	0	7	2	6
Poland	3	2	0	1	3	2	4
Sweden	3	1	0	2	4	6	2
Yugoslavia	3	0	0	3	2	6	0

THIRD PLACE MATCH

Poland 1, Brazil 0

FINAL *Munich*

West Germany 2, Holland 1

West Germany: Maier, Vogts, Schwarzenbeck, Beckenbauer, Breitner, Bonhof, Hoeness, Overath, Grabowski, Muller, Holzenbein.

Holland: Jongbloed, Suurbier, Rijsbergen (De Jong), Haan, Krol, Jansen, Van Hanegem, Neeskens, Rep, Cruyff, Rensenbrink (Van der Kerkhof R.).

Scorers: Breitner *(pen),* Muller for West Germany; Neeskens *(pen)* for Holland. *Leading Scorer:* Lato (Poland) 7.

ARGENTINA 1978

GROUP 1

Italy 2, France 1
Argentina 2, Hungary 1
Italy 3, Hungary 1
Argentina 2, France 1
France 3, Hungary 1
Italy 1, Argentina 0

	P	W	D	L	F	A	Pts
Italy	3	3	0	0	6	2	6
Argentina	3	2	0	1	4	3	4
France	3	1	0	2	5	5	2
Hungary	3	0	0	3	3	8	0

GROUP 2

West Germany 0, Poland 0
Tunisia 3, Mexico 1
Poland 1, Tunisia 0
West Germany 6, Mexico 0
Poland 3, Mexico 1
West Germany 0, Tunisia 0

	P	W	D	L	F	A	Pts
Poland	3	2	1	0	4	1	5
West Germany	3	1	2	0	6	0	4
Tunisia	3	1	1	1	3	2	3
Mexico	3	0	0	3	2	12	0

GROUP 3

Austria 2, Spain 1
Brazil 1, Sweden 1
Austria 1, Sweden 0
Brazil 0, Spain 0
Spain 1, Sweden 0
Brazil 1, Austria 0

	P	W	D	L	F	A	Pts
Austria	3	2	0	1	3	2	4
Brazil	3	1	2	0	2	1	4
Spain	3	1	1	1	2	2	3
Sweden	3	0	1	2	1	3	1

GROUP 4

Peru 3, Scotland 1
Holland 3, Iran 0
Scotland 1, Iran 1
Holland 0, Peru 0
Peru 4, Iran 1
Scotland 3, Holland 2

	P	W	D	L	F	A	Pts
Peru	3	2	1	0	7	2	5
Holland	3	1	1	1	5	3	3
Scotland	3	1	1	1	5	6	3
Iran	3	0	1	2	2	8	1

GROUP A

West Germany 0, Italy 0
Holland 5, Austria 1
Italy 1, Austria 0
Holland 2, West Germany 2
Holland 2, Italy 1
Austria 3, West Germany 2

	P	W	D	L	F	A	Pts
Holland	3	2	1	0	9	4	5
Italy	3	1	1	1	2	2	3
West Germany	3	0	2	1	4	5	2
Austria	3	1	0	2	4	8	2

GROUP B

Brazil 3, Peru 0
Argentina 2, Poland 0
Poland 1, Peru 0
Argentina 0, Brazil 0
Brazil 3, Poland 1
Argentina 6, Peru 0

	P	W	D	L	F	A	Pts
Argentina	3	2	1	0	8	0	5
Brazil	3	2	1	0	6	1	5
Poland	3	1	0	2	2	5	2
Peru	3	0	0	3	0	10	0

THIRD PLACE MATCH

Brazil 2, Italy 1

FINAL *Buenos Aires*

Argentina 3, Holland 1 after extra time

Argentina: Fillol, Passarella, Olguin, Galvan L., Tarantini, Ardiles (Larrosa), Gallego, Ortiz (Houseman), Bertoni, Luque, Kempes.
Holland: Jongbloed, Krol, Poortvliet, Brandts, Jansen (Suurbier), Haan, Neeskens, van der Kerkhof W., Rep (Nanninga), van der Kerkhof R., Rensenbrink.
Scorers: Kempes, Bertoni for Argentina; Nanninga for Holland.
Ref: S. Gonella (Italy).
Leading Scorer: Kempes (Argentina) 6.

SPAIN 1982

GROUP 1

		P	W	D	L	F	A	Pts
Italy 0, Poland 0	Poland	3	1	2	0	5	1	4
Cameroon 0, Peru 0	Italy	3	0	3	0	2	2	3
Italy 1, Peru 1	Cameroon	3	0	3	0	1	1	3
Cameroon 0, Poland 0	Peru	3	0	2	1	2	6	2
Poland 5, Peru 1								
Cameroon 1, Italy 1								

GROUP 2

		P	W	D	L	F	A	Pts
Algeria 2, West Germany 1	West Germany	3	2	0	1	6	3	4
Austria 1, Chile 0	Austria	3	2	0	1	3	1	4
West Germany 4, Chile 1	Algeria	3	2	0	1	5	5	4
Austria 2, Algeria 0	Chile	3	0	0	3	3	8	0
Algeria 3, Chile 2								
West Germany 1, Austria 0								

GROUP 3

		P	W	D	L	F	A	Pts
Belgium 1, Argentina 0	Belgium	3	2	1	0	3	1	5
Hungary 10, El Salvador 1	Argentina	3	2	0	1	6	2	4
Argentina 4, Hungary 1	Hungary	3	1	1	1	12	6	3
Belgium 1, El Salvador 0	El Salvador	3	0	0	3	1	13	0
Belgium 1, Hungary 1								
Argentina 2, El Salvador 0								

GROUP 4

		P	W	D	L	F	A	Pts
England 3, France 1	England	3	3	0	0	6	1	6
Czechoslovakia 1, Kuwait 1	France	3	2	0	1	6	5	4
England 2, Czechoslovakia 0	Czechoslovakia	3	0	2	1	2	4	2
France 4, Kuwait 1	Kuwait	3	0	1	2	2	6	1
Czechoslovakia 1, France 1								
England 1, Kuwait 0								

GROUP 5

		P	W	D	L	F	A	Pts
Honduras 1, Spain 1	N. Ireland	3	1	2	0	2	1	4
N. Ireland 0, Yugoslavia 0	Spain	3	1	1	1	3	2	3
Spain 2, Yugoslavia 1	Yugoslavia	3	1	1	1	2	2	3
Honduras 1, N. Ireland 1	Honduras	3	0	2	1	2	3	2
Yugoslavia 1, Honduras 0								
N. Ireland 1, Spain 0								

GROUP 6

		P	W	D	L	F	A	Pts
Brazil 2, USSR 1	Brazil	3	3	0	0	10	2	6
Scotland 5, New Zealand 2	USSR	3	1	1	1	6	4	3
Brazil 4, Scotland 1	Scotland	3	1	1	1	8	8	3
USSR 3, New Zealand 0	New Zealand	3	0	0	3	2	12	0
Scotland 2, USSR 2								
Brazil 4, New Zealand 0								

GROUP A

Poland 3, Belgium 0
USSR 1, Belgium 0
Poland 0, USSR 0

	P	W	D	L	F	A	Pts
Poland	2	1	1	0	3	0	3
USSR	2	1	1	0	1	0	3
Belgium	2	0	0	2	0	4	0

GROUP B

England 0, West Germany 0
West Germany 2, Spain 1
England 0, Spain 0

	P	W	D	L	F	A	Pts
West Germany	2	1	1	0	2	1	3
England	2	0	2	0	0	0	2
Spain	2	0	1	2	1	2	1

GROUP C

Italy 2, Argentina 1
Brazil 3, Argentina 1
Italy 3, Brazil 2

	P	W	D	L	F	A	Pts
Italy	2	2	0	0	5	3	4
Brazil	2	1	0	1	5	4	2
Argentina	2	0	0	2	2	5	0

GROUP D

France 1, Austria 0
Austria 2, N. Ireland 2
France 4, N. Ireland 1

	P	W	D	L	F	A	Pts
France	2	2	0	0	5	1	4
Austria	2	0	1	1	2	3	1
N. Ireland	2	0	1	1	3	6	1

SEMI-FINALS

Italy 2, Poland 0
West Germany 3, France 3 (after extra time) West Germany won 5-4 on penalties

THIRD PLACE MATCH

Poland 3, France 2

FINAL *Madrid*

Italy 3, West Germany 1

Italy: Zoff, Gentile, Scirea, Collovati, Cabrini, Bergoni, Tardelli, Oriali, Conti, Rossi, Graziani, Altobelli (Causio).

West Germany: Schumacher, Kaltz, Stielike, Förster K-H, Briegel, Dremmler (Hrubesch), Forster B, Breitner, Littbarski, Rummenigge (Muller), Fischer.

Scorers: Rossi, Tardelli, Altobelli for Italy; Breitner for West Germany.

Ref: A. Coelho (Brazil)

Leading Scorer: Rossi (Italy) 6.

HOW THEY LINE UP

GROUP A		**GROUP D**	
(Puebla, Mexico City)		*(Guadalajara, Monterrey)*	
ITALY	Argentina	BRAZIL	Spain
Bulgaria	South Korea	N. Ireland	Algeria

GROUP B		**GROUP E**	
(Mexico City, Toluca)		*(Querétaro, Neza)*	
MEXICO	Paraguay	WEST GERMANY	Uruguay
Belgium	Iraq	Scotland	Denmark

GROUP C		**GROUP F**	
(León, Irapuato)		*(Monterrey, Guadalajara)*	
FRANCE	USSR	POLAND	England
Hungary	Canada	Portugal	Morocco

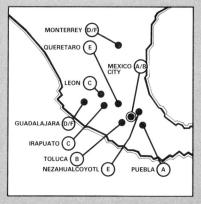

Smile when you say that: England manager Bobby Robson and FA Secretary Ted Croker construct a happy face after the bad news of Monterrey

WHO PLAYS WHEN – AND WHERE

GROUP A

Saturday, 31 May	**Bulgaria**	**v Italy**	Mexico City *(Azteca)*
Monday, 2 June	**Argentina**	**v South Korea**	Mexico City *Olímpico '68)*
Thursday, 5 June	**Italy**	**v Argentina**	Puebla *(Cuauhtémoc)*
	South Korea	**v Bulgaria**	Mexico City *(Olímpico '68)*
Tuesday, 10 June	**South Korea**	**v Italy**	Puebla *(Cuauhtémoc)*
	Argentina	**v Bulgaria**	Mexico City *(Olímpico '68)*

GROUP B

Tuesday, 3 June	**Belgium**	**v Mexico**	Mexico City *(Azteca)*
Wednesday, 4 June	**Paraguay**	**v Iraq**	Toluca *(Toluca)*
Saturday, 7 June	**Mexico**	**v Paraguay**	Mexico City *(Azteca)*
Sunday, 8 June	**Iraq**	**v Belgium**	Toluca *(Toluca)*
Wednesday, 11 June	**Iraq**	**v Mexico**	Mexico City *(Azteca)*
	Paraguay	**v Belgium**	Toluca *(Toluca)*

GROUP C

Sunday, 1 June	**Canada**	**v France**	León *(León)*
Monday, 2 June	**USSR**	**v Hungary**	Irapuato *(Irapuato)*
Thursday, 5 June	**France**	**v USSR**	León *(León)*
Friday, 6 June	**Hungary**	**v Canada**	Irapuato *(Irapuato)*
Monday, 9 June	**Hungary**	**v France**	León *(León)*
	USSR	**v Canada**	Irapuato *(Irapuato)*

GROUP D

Sunday, 1 June	**Spain**	**v Brazil**	Guadalajara *(Jalisco)*
Tuesday, 3 June	**Algeria**	**v N. Ireland**	Guadalajara *(3 de Marzo)*
Friday, 6 June	**Brazil**	**v Algeria**	Guadalajara *(Jalisco)*
Saturday, 7 June	**N. Ireland**	**v Spain**	Guadalajara *(3 de Marzo)*
Thursday, 12 June	**N. Ireland**	**v Brazil**	Guadalajara *(Jalisco)*
	Algeria	**v Spain**	Monterrey *(Tecnológico)*

GROUP E

Wednesday, 4 June	**Uruguay**	**v W. Germany**	Querétaro *(Corregidora)*
	Scotland	**v Denmark**	Nezahualcoyotl *(Neza '86)*
Sunday, 8 June	**W. Germany**	**v Scotland**	Querétaro *(Corregidora)*
	Denmark	**v Uruguay**	Nezahualcoyotl *(Neza '86)*
Friday, 13 June	**Denmark**	**v W. Germany**	Querétaro *(Corregidora)*
	Scotland	**v Uruguay**	Nezahualcoyotl *(Neza '86)*

GROUP F

Monday, 2 June	**Morocco** v **Poland**	Monterrey *(Universitario)*
Tuesday, 3 June	**Portugal** v **England**	Monterrey *(Tecnológico)*
Friday, 6 June	**England** v **Morocco**	Monterrey *(Tecnológico)*
Saturday, 7 June	**Poland** v **Portugal**	Monterrey *(Universitario)*
Wednesday, 11 June	**Portugal** v **Morocco**	Guadalajara *(3 de Marzo)*
	England v **Poland**	Monterrey *(Universitario)*

The two top teams in each group qualify for the knock-out second round, along with the four third-place teams with the best record.

SECOND ROUND

Sunday, 15 June	**B winner v A/C/D third**	Mexico City *(Azteca)*	I
	C winner v A/B/F third	León *(León)*	II
Monday, 16 June	**A winner v C/D/E third**	Puebla *(Cuahtémoc)*	III
	D winner v B/E/F third	Guadalajara *(Jalisco)*	IV
Tuesday, 17 June	**A second v C second**	Mexico City *(Olímpico '68)*	V
	F winner v E second	Monterrey *(Universitario)*	VI
Wednesday, 18 June	**F second v B second**	Mexico City *(Azteca)*	VII
	E winner v D second	Querétaro *(Corregidora)*	VIII

QUARTER-FINALS

Saturday, 21 June	**IV v V**	Guadalajara *(Jalisco)*	A
	I v VI	Monterrey *(Universitario)*	B
Sunday, 22 June	**II v VIII**	Puebla *(Cuauhtémoc)*	C
	III v VII	Mexico City *(Azteca)*	D

SEMI-FINALS

Wednesday, 25 June	**C v D**	Mexico City *(Azteca)*
	A v B	Guadalajara *(Jalisco)*

THIRD/FOURTH PLACE

Saturday, 28 June	**Semi-final losers**	Puebla *(Cuauhtémoc)*

FINAL

Sunday, 29 June	**Semi-final winners**	Mexico City *(Azteca)*

Rest days: Saturday, 14 June, Thursday, 19 June, Friday, 20 June, Monday, 23 June, Tuesday, 24 June, Thursday, 26 June, Friday, 27 June.

GROUP A

	P	W	D	L	F	A	Pts
Italy							
Bulgaria							
Argentina							
S. Korea							

Bulgaria ____, Italy ____
Argentina ____, S. Korea ____
Italy ____, Argentina ____
S. Korea ____, Bulgaria ____
S. Korea ____, Italy ____
Argentina ____, Bulgaria ____

GROUP B

	P	W	D	L	F	A	Pts
Mexico							
Belgium							
Paraguay							
Iraq							

Belgium ____, Mexico ____
Paraguay ____, Iraq ____
Mexico ____, Paraguay ____
Iraq ____, Belgium ____
Iraq ____, Mexico ____
Paraguay ____, Belgium ____

GROUP C

	P	W	D	L	F	A	Pts
France							
Hungary							
USSR							
Canada							

Canada ____, France ____
USSR ____, Hungary ____
France ____, USSR ____
Hungary ____, Canada ____
Hungary ____, France ____
USSR ____, Canada ____

GROUP D

	P	W	D	L	F	A	Pts
Brazil							
N.Ireland							
Spain							
Algeria							

Spain ____, Brazil ____
Algeria ____, N.Ireland ____
Brazil ____, Algeria ____
N.Ireland ____, Spain ____
N.Ireland ____, Brazil ____
Algeria ____, Spain ____

GROUP E

	P	W	D	L	F	A	Pts
W. Germany							
Scotland							
Uruguay							
Denmark							

Uruguay ____, W. Germany ____
Scotland ____, Denmark ____
W. Germany ____, Scotland ____
Denmark ____, Uruguay ____
Denmark ____, W. Germany ____
Scotland ____, Uruguay ____

GROUP F

	P	W	D	L	F	A	Pts
Poland							
Portugal							
England							
Morocco							

Morocco ____, Poland ____
Portugal ____, England ____
England ____, Morocco ____
Poland ____, Portugal ____
Portugal ____, Morocco ____
England ____, Poland ____

SECOND ROUND

	v	
	v	
	v	
	v	
	v	
	v	
	v	
	v	

QUARTER-FINALS

	v	
	v	
	v	
	v	

SEMI-FINALS

	v	
	v	

THIRD/FOURTH PLACE

	v	

FINAL

$$\underline{\qquad 1 \qquad}$$

$$\underline{\quad 2 \quad} \qquad \underline{\quad 3 \quad} \qquad \underline{\quad 4 \quad} \qquad \underline{\quad 5 \quad}$$

$$\underline{\quad 6 \quad} \qquad \underline{\quad 7 \quad} \qquad \underline{\quad 8 \quad}$$

$$\underline{\quad 9 \quad} \qquad \underline{\quad 10 \quad} \qquad \underline{\quad 11 \quad}$$

Kick-off, 12 noon, Sunday 29 June, Mexico City

$$\underline{\quad 11 \quad} \qquad \underline{\quad 10 \quad} \qquad \underline{\quad 9 \quad}$$

$$\underline{\quad 8 \quad} \qquad \underline{\quad 7 \quad} \qquad \underline{\quad 6 \quad}$$

$$\underline{\quad 5 \quad} \qquad \underline{\quad 4 \quad} \qquad \underline{\quad 3 \quad} \qquad \underline{\quad 2 \quad}$$

$$\underline{\qquad 1 \qquad}$$

Referee———— Half-time score———— Result ————